SAVE THE CAT!®
BLAKE'S
BLOGS

More Information and Inspiration for Writers

BLAKE SNYDER

Published by *Save the Cat!*® Press

Curator and Editor:
Rich Kaplan

Cover Photo:
Rebecca Tull Yates

Cover and Interior Book Design:
Gina Mansfield

The author acknowledges
the copyright owners of the motion pictures
from which single frames
have been used in this book
for purposes of commentary
under the Fair Use Doctrine.

Planes, Trains and Automobiles 1987
Michael Clayton 2007
Slumdog Millionaire 2008
There Will Be Blood 2007

The blog posts herein were originally published on
www.savethecat.com from 2005 – 2009.
They have been edited for this book.

ISBN 978-0-9841576-7-9

Like you, I have wanted to be a writer all my life. Writing is my passion and the best fun I've ever had. I have made my best discoveries about this through many writing partnerships. Talking to each other about what we discover is the only way to learn. My name is Blake Snyder. I am your humble servant. I am an "expert" in this business only in that I can admit that as much experience as I've had, every day offers the possibility of learning something new. It has always been my motto, "There is plenty for every-body!" — meaning that there is enough success to go around. By helping you win, I win too. We all do. And that is the only way to become not only a better writer, but to make the world a better place.

So let's get going.

December 9, 2005

TABLE OF CONTENTS

INTRODUCTION

The blog posts in this book have been carefully curated and edited from Blake's originals. We have selected posts that we believe are timeless, resonating as powerfully today as on the day Blake wrote them. In addition, we've created 10 chapters in which we've bundled posts according to categories, to simplify your search for the information and inspiration that were Blake's hallmarks.

Enjoy!

Rich Kaplan

PROLOGUE

March 6, 2009

Excellence has rules; what are ours? As screenwriters vitally interested in succeeding, what frame of mind must we assume to rise above the average, push ourselves and our scripts to a higher level, and greet each hurdle as a chance to improve ourselves and our work? What can we do — right now, today — to step up to the challenge, committed to strive for excellence in thought, word, and deed?

Here is a starting point:

The Ten Commandments of Screenwriting Excellence

1. Thou Shalt Use "The Rules" Not Be Used By Them — Who better to create improvement within an industry than those who understand "The Rules" by which it operates? Communication on a mass scale requires knowledge of what works and why, but it doesn't mean we have to rely solely on what worked the day before. Knowing why "the poster" is vital, why targeting an audience is key, and how to be clear in our communication is our ammunition. We must have a slight smile that comes from insider knowledge, but use that knowledge like a jujitsu expert, always in command of what is required, but never subordinate to the demand. Only knowing "The Rules" allows this. Blunt force, storming the barricades, tearing down the system is a step backward. It is a system worth preserving — one we will miss if it ever is taken away — so we must save it by helping it not destroy itself. We must accept the responsibility to be the masters of it.

2. **Thou Shalt Always Move The Art Forward** — Cliché is our enemy. But to be better than cliché, we must embrace it, know it intimately, and at the last minute, insist on the new. Stories progress over the years, they are the same... but different for our age. Learning what came before is vital to avoid trodding over old territory. Every genre has its historic high and low points, key turns, break-throughs in form, and creators who insisted on nothing less than shattering the tired and old. You have a genre, a type of story you love to tell. It is a story that has a long tradition, riddled with clichés which — at the time — were breathtaking new advances. Now is the time to find your contribution, to break with what came before, but to honor the tradition of your genre by knowing it inside and out and respecting its contribution to now.

3. **Thou Shalt Insist On Meaning** — Ask any writer of genre fiction — or high art — and you will discover the secret of success for both is the same: finding the thing in any story that inspires YOU. And that means insisting that in every story we tell — even an assignment we don't "like" or is not ours — we search for, and insist we "find our way into," what it's "about." To do so, we must lay our message into the B Story. Do not proclaim your Good Intentions in the A Story. Bury it subtlety, and powerfully beneath the surface in the "helper story" that helps your hero, and us, learn the lesson. Billboarding your Good Intentions in the A Story is a bore, but not addressing meaning in the B Story is half-finished work. To find meaning is to find inspiration, and only art snobs refuse to find it in assignments and genres they think are "beneath them." The truth is we can find meaning in any story, and it is up to us to insist we find it in every story we tell.

4. **Thou Shalt Not Take "Good Enough" For An Answer** — There are lots of scenes, ideas, plot points, and motifs that are "good enough." That'll "hold 'em" you might catch yourself thinking. But

if you get the sense you can do better, if you have a feeling your "place holder" is becoming permanent, stop! Try again, push yourself for the better one. All of this is about developing a gut that insists on quality beyond "good enough." "I can do better!" should always be our motto, no matter how intent we are on "locking down" story points, being satisfied with what merely works, and finishing the assignment. There is always time for making it better; there is always a place on my team for any writer who is still emailing suggestions on how to improve, buff up, or find creative solutions that lift the story or scene beyond just "that'll be okay."

5. **Thou Shalt Disappear From Thy Script** — Do not be too cute or too showoffy about yourself. If you find yourself thinking, "They'll really be impressed with my screenwriting here," you're wrong. Your voice, yes; your style, sure; your take on the Truth, absolutely. But if YOU are all over your screenplay, intruding on your script because you want to make extra sure the audience knows it was written — by you! — odds are it's at the cost of the real heroes of your tale — the characters you have created that are really telling this story. "Look at me!" should not be our subtext; "Look at this great story and great characters!" should. We are not the story, our story is. For screenwriters this is particularly challenging because very few appear to have a "voice" or a "style" that's obvious on the screen. If you want to be known, if your desire is fame, the best way to achieve it is as a great storyteller, with a reputation for telling a story, not being the star of it.

6. **Thou Shalt Not Suffer** — Part of the guide to success is joy. It doesn't have to hurt to be great work; in fact, often the easy ones come easily for a reason — because they are direct from a Higher Power right onto the page. Even if you're off, and your work requires re-working, it should be a game — fun, delightful, joyful, always an adventure! Many writers confuse hard work for overwork, and hang on to the number of their rewrites as a badge of courage

and proof that their suffering makes the work better. Not true. If you are not loving this, if this is drudgery, if you aren't thrilled with finding new ways to do your job, and learning new tricks to do it better — and being always curious about the process — consider another line of work. There's a difference between intensity and masochism for masochism's sake. Having fun and feeling challenged by the work in a positive way is the only way to know you are on the right track.

7. **Thou Shalt Be A Good Listener** — Moviemaking is a team sport, and playing well with others is an unsung talent. It starts with hearing feedback. But listening does not mean you discount or discriminate against those giving feedback. "Civilians" are often far more brilliant than seasoned pros who give notes by rote, or by what has worked in the past and may not work now. Listening to them all, and hearing what they say, gives us the perspective to make our work better. This is a gift of unparalleled importance. In the headlong rush to communicate, in the blinders-on mission to get our brilliance down on the page — as important as that is — our job must be tempered by a calmer, "tools down" moment, when we can actually hear how our very important points are going over. Sometimes we are right, but sometimes we are dead wrong, and there's only one way to find out: listening to everyone who reads or responds to our work.

8. **Thou Shalt Mix It Up** — I have never been a fan of research. I am a fan of letting our imaginations tell a story that can be more real than anything "accurate." But I am against the stale life, and a staunch opponent of what I like to call "Bungalow Fever" that many a screenwriter is plague to, and for which there is only one cure: Get away from your computer, leave the house, and go out and live!

Hobbies, service to others, charity work, travel, a sport we love, even other kinds of writing, all contribute to a fuller and better world view — and a head full of fresh and exciting images we can't wait to talk about when we return to our cursors! The cause of sameness, lack of creativity, and boredom at the Cineplex is the echo chamber that is a parochial POV. Get some fresh air, for the body and for the mind, and fresh scripts will be the result!

9. **Thou Shalt Be Pleased When Others Succeed** — "There is plenty for everybody!" This must be our mantra and our guiding light. So when we read of a sale of a script in our genre, or learn that a contemporary, or even a friend, has found success, we should feel fantastic! Any time one of our own "takes a dollar from the man," it is a victory for us all. We must get in the habit of buying and sending lots of Hallmark cards of congratulations to our fellows. Their victory means ours is coming. But more than that, we need to be comrades in arms, to help each other succeed, not secretly be jealous of someone else's progress. For that way lies the desert, the unfertile and scorched earth life of barren isolation. And it flies in the face of what we are striving for: excellence. Learn from others. Discover what they did that you can do to make your next script better. Admire excellence in others and laud them for it. For excellence in others is ours, too!

10. **Thou Shalt Be The Best** — One sure way to achieve excellence is to claim it. Be proud of your genre and be a proud spokesman for it because you know you are at the leading edge of its improvement! Whatever one you've picked, master it, push the boundaries, bend the rules — or break them. With expertise comes... boredom. Good! So challenge yourself to go beyond, and constantly push yourself. By studying every aspect of your specialty, from the history of movies yours derives from, and how a movie from the '40s begat the one in the '90s which begat what you're working on, you see that pushing the trends comes from formal knowledge of what came before: Know what worked and what didn't and why, and always push to make your contribution, dare I say it, historic. It doesn't have to win an Academy Award* to earn the respect of your peers, those

in the trenches who embody real success. The veterans, the steely pros, those who aren't the Monday morning quarterbacks sneering at Hollywood (out of jealousy) but its working creatives know what you've done and what your effort means. And they're the ones who count most.

Like I say, we are at a crossroads. We must improve. We must do better. This is our chance! Let's do it.

March 6, 2009

CHAPTER 1

Blake's Blog / June 23, 2008
*"A confusing idea is like a chicken omelet:
you can't quite put your finger on exactly
what's wrong."*

IDEAS AND CONCEPTS

CONCEPT, CONCEPT, CONCEPT
July 11, 2006

I have read a lot of scripts lately that are well-written, show passion and thought, and yet ultimately I must get on the phone or write an email to its author or authors with not so pretty news.

Why?

No concept.

Despite being very funny or dramatic or exciting, there is no over-arching idea at play that can arouse attention or interest.

And the really sad part is, this is so easy to overcome BEFORE you write 110 pages of script.

It is the premise of *STC!* and the grounding of all my efforts out there teaching: please, please have a good pitch!

Because if you don't, no matter how great the writing is, you will have a helluva time getting it set up.

Yes, this goes for Indies, too, and blockbusters, and everything in between. Because no matter how earnest you are about your work, it boils down to communicating an idea succinctly.

Here are some hints that the idea you are working on is not the high concept sale you think it might be:

1. You haven't told anybody the idea but have kept it to yourself. Why? Well, it's so good someone might steal it!

2. When asked to tell about the movie you're writing at the Fourth of July picnic, you tell it from the Fade In: and you go on, and on, and on about it, all the while waiting to get to the good part, which is in there, you swear!

3. The idea you're working is based on certain "conditions," the return of the popularity of ice hockey, or casting Jack Nicholson, or the ever-burgeoning spread in the knowledge of and interest in stamp collecting. These conditions are excuses. And shouldn't be. Blaming not selling a script due to Jack not being attached or the reader not "getting it" is hubris. It's either a great movie everyone gets — or it's not.

If any of this sounds familiar, beware! Check your concept. Make sure it really satisfies the 4 elements of a successful logline as out-lined in *Save the Cat!,* and for God's sake, pitch it. A lot. Trust me, no one is going to steal your idea. And the sad truth is, once you expose that idea to air, you may well watch its shimmer fade like fool's gold.

But better to have that happen BEFORE you toil away on your 110+ pages than after.

Know the condition of your screenplay first by knowing and get-ting great reaction on its concept — It's the law!

ONE IDEA
March 26, 2009

I was working with a screenwriter this week who made me think of something I say in class a lot:

4 + 4 ELEMENTS OF
EVERY SUCCESSFUL LOGLINE

THE 4 BASICS:

A *type* of **Protagonist** – Whose story is this, and who will we be following in this adventure? Ask yourself, "What's wrong with my hero?" Provide us with a sense of what ails him or her emotionally, and not just physically. *What is your protagonist's flaw?*

A *type* of **Antagonist** – Who is stopping the protagonist from achieving his or her goal and why? What drives your antagonist that tells us that he or she will not make things easy for your hero? Why is the antagonist your hero's worst nightmare?

Conflict – If you don't have conflict, you don't have a story. Make certain that you tell us what your hero wants, what your hero needs, and what is stopping him or her from getting it.

An Open-Ended Question – Don't give it all away. The logline is just a teaser of what to expect – not a summary. If you keep your reader hanging on for more, there's a good chance he or she will *want* to read your script.

PLUS 4 MORE:

Irony – Your logline must be in some way *ironic* and *emotionally involving* – a dramatic situation that is like an itch you have to scratch. "Irony" is surprise, an O. Henry-like twist, something that intrigues and delights us.

A Compelling Mental Picture must *bloom in your mind*. A whole movie must be implied in your logline, often including a time frame. Use a few select words that create good visuals, set pieces, and thematic possibilities.

Audience and Cost – Your logline must demarcate your film's tone, its target audience, and a sense of cost – three factors potential buyers will want to know upfront. Answer this question: Who is this story for?

A Killer Title – The one-two punch of a good logline *must* include a great title, one that "says what it is" and does so in a clever way – and yet, is not "on the nose."

SAVE THE CAT!® TEACHING MATERIALS

Save the Cat!® Workshop hand-out on What Makes a Great Logline.

A movie is about "one idea."

I was reminded that in his book, *Your Screenplay Sucks*, my pal Will Akers says the very same thing.

To many this precept is confusing. And feels "restricting." *I am brilliant! I can weave many ideas through my screenplay. I will not be "dumbed down" into limiting myself and my creativity!* you will protest.

And I agree.

But one idea, well told, is actually the way to make your script more meaningful. Finding the "one idea" makes your story spine stronger. Yours must be a tale in which we "follow the bouncing ball" of a hero who changes from beginning to end. Your hero must learn a lesson — pick one — and you are telling us what that is by clearly planting your Theme Stated up front... and tying it to the "lesson learned" at the end.

But as stated in *Save the Cat!* — and whenever I get to be face to face with you in class, or while working on your script with you — once you find that Theme, and can stick to it, you can weave in many different skeins of meaning! A movie is a debate, the pros and cons of a particular point of view or way of living. As long as it works off of your main theme, you can be as freewheeling as you like and have confidence that you will not lose your audience, or diminish the power of your thematic intention by diluting your story.

The "one idea" rule also helps you decide if it's a love story... or a thriller. And don't you wish more moviemakers would decide this? We can understand multiple levels of meaning, as long as your intention as the writer is clear. Sticking to the "one idea per movie" rule helps us focus on what we're really saying.

WHERE'S THE IRONY?
August 21, 2008

One thing that *Save the Cat!* is best known for, and no other screenwriting book really discusses, is "the idea." That may be because I have always been "the poster guy," the writer who loves concept and to whom other writers come to see if their idea works, and if not how they can make it work.

What is your pitch, your logline, your encapsulation of the brand new movie idea that you love?

And how can we communicate that idea to the listener or reader of our pitch or logline without losing them?

We see it! We're excited! We are inspired!

Why aren't they?

Among the deficiencies in an idea that doesn't grab me is No Stakes — basically there is nothing riding on this story for your hero. Another is Tone. If I can't tell if your idea is a drama or a comedy, trouble! Many times I have written back to a writer saying:" Ha! Hilarious idea!" only to be told it's a searing drama. Oops! But believe it or not, that's not my fault, that's yours. If you aren't indicating somehow what the tone of this idea is, you have fallen short.

The fix of an idea that doesn't grab me — comedy or drama — almost always is to find the "irony" of it. What gets our attention, what is the "hook," the "sizzle" of an idea? What's "ironic" about *Erin Brockovich* is not the plot, which finds a crusader exposing the wrongs of a powerful company, but the fact that the person doing the crusading is the very last person on Earth who would be called to this duty. Irony is not only the "sizzle," it hints at the transformation of the hero, and the size of the challenge as well.

Your idea is the same.

Where's the irony of your idea? That's not only what gets our attention, but what hints at a story about a hero that changes. These can all be indicated in your pitch or logline, little clues that give us a clue about what's in your fevered imagination.

And saying it, right up front, grabbing our attention and luring us in for more, is the first step in inviting me into the darkness of your air-conditioned movie theater and finding a center seat in anticipation of a great experience!

COMING UP WITH A GREAT MOVIE IDEA!
August 2, 2006

I just got off the phone talking to a writer I am working with, a very talented guy who is looking to come up with a brand new movie idea.

How, he asked, can this be done? Like me, he has a bunch of ideas he has been working on, but none have that spark that makes us anxious to pitch to anyone.

We all know that the killer title (*Snakes on a Plane*, *40-Year-Old-Virgin*) plus the killer concept equals the one-two punch we are all looking for. But how do we generate these?

Here are some exercises I suggested and ones I use when I am coming up with new ideas:

1. **The Movie Star Game**. Though you won't get these actors to star in your movie, think of the next movie that Tom Cruise needs to do. What about Meg Ryan? Reese Witherspoon? Brad Pitt? If you were managing the careers of these actors, or any others you can think of, what movie would you write for them? And while you're at it, why not make that idea outrageous? Think outside the five-sided trapezoid. And at the end of this brainstorming, when you remove the star from the actual logline, what you may have is a movie that suits many leading actors.

2. **Mix and Match**. Heard a great pitch in the seminar we held here in LA two weekends ago. *Grumpy Old Men* meets *Road Trip*. That was the pitch — and I get it immediately. It strikes me that going through a movie listing book like "Leonard Maltin's Movie Guide" and mixing and matching outrageous combinations might be a great way to springboard something new. I know I have tried this, and again, you'd be surprised at the great ideas that result.

3. **The T-Bar Method**. I've talked about this before. Draw a T on a piece of paper. On one side make a list of protagonists, on the other

a matching list of antagonists who might be in direct opposition to your heroes. Example: A recently divorced local preacher is the protagonist; the antagonist is the female owner of a massage parlor that's just moved to town. Keep adding to the list, keep giving the opposition the most conflict you can, and see what story develops from it. Try a different T-bar for different styles of movies. It's particularly good if you're trying to come up with a romantic comedy and looking for new types of male and female leads in conflict.

4. **Title First**. Finally, when it comes to finding a killer title, maybe start with one that already exists and figure out a story to match? This is how I got going on *Nuclear Family*. I began with the title, then figured out an ironic twist that made the title that much better. Point of all this is: Don't be so logical. Try to break out from the ordinary and get free of beating on the same old loglines you've been working on that just don't pop. Stand on your head, figuratively speaking, and see it all in a new way.

THE PRIMAL PIECE
July 24, 2009

Overheard at the place where I get my hair cut:

"I think it's about comedians. It seems okay. Then I saw that Adam Sandler is, I guess, dying or something. It looks really good."

This was a conversation about the upcoming Judd Apatow movie, *Funny People*. Yes we are all going to see it, and I personally can't wait. But just because *I'm* interested doesn't mean everyone is.

What I found in that overheard bit of conversation was something fascinating... and a little scary.

If we're lucky enough to have our movies bought and made, we will eventually find ourselves in the hands of the Marketing Department. There is an array of weapons at their disposal to get the word out about our film: A series of ads on TV, the trailer or two, a Behind the Scenes look on HBO. And there will hopefully be a message that explains "What is it?" One that is clear... and compelling.

But what it boils down to is: Do we get it? Do we pull from the 20-30 second message in a day of a million 20-30 second messages, the thing that makes us go? Because all you really can get across is the barest semblance of the plot, the cast, a general feeling of whether or not it's interesting.

What travels best is: primal. We sorta had them there with the comedian description, everyone likes *Funny People*, don't they? But what got this person's attention that I heard over the blow dryer, the part that stuck, was the primal part: Adam might be dying. And that made all the difference. Now there are stakes for him — and us. Now there's a plot. Now I'll go check it out.

What's the primal piece in the movie you're writing? What essential element will catch the attention of busy audiences? A pregnancy, a divorce, the impossible chase to find love? The caveman song of survival, hunger, death, father, mother, sister, brother, wife, child?

When we ask "What is it?" we not only need the hook — and that has to be fantastic!! — we will also need a primal reason to stay put and listen. Finding your primal piece not only helps you focus on what your story is saying, but helps communicate an idea that even the busiest cavemen "get."

SUPER BOWL ADS – *STC!* 101
February 5, 2007

As you all know by now, I look for story elements in everything. And there were some great ones to be found in the best commercials of yesterday's Super Bowl.

Why is it that the need to communicate an idea quickly forces storytellers — and that's who creative ad execs are — to narrow their focus to the most primal conflicts and use the most basic emotions to get our attention? Because those primal ads work — instantly and perpetually. All storytellers should take note.

My favorite was a Doritos ad. This is the one which I believe was submitted by a non-professional as part of a contest the company sponsored. It involves a boy driving down the street, spotting a pretty girl, and crashing his car — only to have the girl come to his rescue and reveal she is just as accident-prone. It was a story told in four flashes, each labeled as a different quality of the corn chip — "spicy," "bold," "crunchy" — and yet in 30 seconds it told a whole story. Alpha-omega. With an opening image and final image that showed a "transformation" and a topic we all relate to: sex.

Fantastic.

My other favorite — for Chevy — was yet another *Save the Cat!*® example, but this was more about Save the Auto Assembly Plant Robot. Here a yellow, and amazingly anthropomorphic, assembly-line automaton dreams it gets fired and sent out into the street to find work. The variations on this sad little guy trying to make his way as a fast-food speaker box and a condo open-house huckster were hilarious and very nearly poignant. Thank God it was all a dream, but when he woke up, he was back in the plant ready to go to work and give his all to make Chevy the best.

In other fun and notable commercials, we had a lost dog on the street who gets turned into a Dalmatian on a Budweiser truck, and two guys arguing over a beer by playing "Rock, Paper, Scissors" — only to have one get beaned with an actual rock. And there was a trio of pet store animals who couldn't quite get the difference between a computer mouse and a real one.

In all of these, we are immediately thrust into a primal conflict over the most basic things: survival, sex, hunger — all things a "caveman" would understand! And so do we.

Each ad is an amazing display of creativity.

But how does it help us screenwriters?

I think there is value in studying all storytelling. And there is great power in giving ourselves limits within which to work — like the confinement of a 30-second spot — or a 15-point structure outline called the BS2.

It also shows that creativity can be lofty and mind-blowing but communication must hit us at the most basic level to work. If we put as much thought into each of the scenes of our scripts that goes into each commercial, we'd be way ahead. And if we always remember that our job as storytellers is to grab and keep a viewer's attention, we will begin to see that the primal forces at the core of every story we tell is the key to its success.

SUPER BOWL ADS 2008: STORIES THAT RESONATE
February 4, 2008

The Super Bowl lived up to its name this year. The stunning, come-from-behind victory of the New York Giants was like something out of a movie. But in addition to being riveted to that underdog story, I was entranced, as I am every year, by the commercials that ran during the football classic.

We can learn about storytelling from any type of communication, and the opportunity to reach so many people at the same time (this was the most watched Super Bowl ever) is rare in the Target Market Era.

How did this year's batch of creativity fare?

Overall, the spots were less spectacular and less memorable than in years past. But there were still a few that grabbed me. And the ones that worked best were those that leaned on the principles of classic storytelling as outlined in the book with the cat on the cover.

I talk in *Save the Cat!* about the importance of "primal." When you pitch me your movie idea, it had better grab my attention at a cave-man level. This is why movies like *Meet the Parents*, about a man visiting his future in-laws for the first time... works! As a caveman, I get that situation and no one has to explain what's on the line. It's why *Jaws* is such a powerful story template, because the prime directive "Don't... get... eaten!" is one they don't have to teach you in school.

In many ways the challenge of a screenwriter is very similar to that of an advertising copywriter, with the same layers of higher-ups (or clients) to appease to put one's ideas across. But this task is even more immediate when you only have 30 seconds to get to the primal... and tell a story that resonates. And we saw many great examples:

HITS

The best of the bunch was the perennial Budweiser ad in which a horse doesn't make the famous Clydesdale team... until his buddy, the Dalmation, puts him through his paces. It's not only an ode to Rocky but a familiar parable. The striving to succeed, to do our best, and the deeper stirring of friendship and "not giving up" are all on display... along with some funny anthropomorphic CGI... not to mention hitting every one of the beats of the BS2!

Thirst is primal. And so is competition — even when the thirsty ones in question are inanimate balloons. So when the Macy's Day parade floats depicting Underdog, and Stewie from *Family Guy*, go chasing after a blow up Coca-Cola bottle through the concrete canyons of New York ... only to lose out to a kinder, gentler Charlie Brown... we get that, too.

But perhaps the most bizarre, and memorable, primal commercial was for careerbuilders.com which saw a dazed and daydreaming employee "follow her heart," literally, as it pops out of her chest — still beating! — and crawls up to her boss's desk to announce: "I quit!" It was dream-like — and spot-on. Isn't this the yearning for a better life that all us daydreaming Neanderthals can understand?

Stories that resonate — that's our job. They can be found anywhere, and we should always be on the lookout for examples of what works and what doesn't.

HIGH CONCEPT RULES
April 23, 2009

2009 has seen a boom at the box office.

And it's been a lesson for anyone interested in what "high concept" means.

The movies that have done well satisfy everything we imply by this term. Take a look at the $100 million+ hits (all except one which just opened) that have "surprised" so many since January 1.

Paul Blart: Mall Cop, *Taken*, *Monsters vs. Aliens*, *Fast and Furious* and *17 Again* are movies that have different tones, fall into different genres and target audiences — but also have a lot in common:

Original ideas — Some screenwriter, or team thereof, sat down and thought it up. And though *Fast and Furious* is the fourth in the franchise, it too started life as an original not based on any other source.

Says "what it is" — These movies each tell us in the poster and the title what each movie is "about."

Easy to explain — Whether we like the idea or not, each has a premise we can pitch.

Fresh — "*Die Hard* in a Mall." That's my pitch for *Paul Blart: Mall Cop*. Creators gave us "the same thing only different," just when I thought the last *Die Hard* in a movie had been made. Guess again.

Two Worlds in Collision — It's there in the title of *Monsters vs. Aliens*.

One thing that catches our attention as an audience is conflict. The bigger the better. And when we see worlds in collision, best!

The term "high concept" is still unclear to me. I first heard it in relation to Michael Eisner and Jeffrey Katzenberg at Disney in the early '80s. The term meant that such a movie was "easy to see" and understand from its poster.

During my first trip to the UK, I saw that the BBC had a website that allowed viewers to listen to the albums of "100 Unsigned Rock Bands." So when I dipped into the list, "dropping the needle" on song after song, what was I listening for?

I was listening for a 'hook" — something that made me want to keep listening! We can learn a lot from this and from "High Concept." No matter what our story, we have to start by getting attention. The means of getting our stories out there is easy — but will anybody "drop the needle" on us — and stay?

Our job is to make sure they do by creating concepts we can tell, that intrigue, that "travel" because their themes are universal. For studios, writers, and creators who love "high concept," it is our time to shine.

P.S. One of the movies I saw recently that I liked a lot was *Fighting*, produced by Kevin Misher. Really interesting performances by Terrence Howard and Channing Tatum, and several standout cameo roles. What's the pitch? It's *Rocky* for the millennium, with a little bit of *Midnight Cowboy* thrown in. Good stuff.

SPIDERING
May 7, 2007

Well, the opening weekend of *Spider-Man 3* is history, and it appears that the blasting out onto 12,000 screens this weekend is great news for box office, but bad news for storytelling.

I am thrilled when Hollywood makes money, but from the sound of it, this marketing approach was based on trying to get all the money they could before reaction to the movie itself set in.

This is one of several techniques producers use when they know their product isn't up to snuff:

1. A huge opening day blowout on as many screens as possible...

2. The holding back of a movie from reviewers until after the movie premieres...

3. An ad campaign that reports the status of actors in it as either a winner of or nominated for an Academy Award® (a wag of a producer once told me that when they roll out a long list of "Starring Academy Award® winner ____" it's akin to saying bring a pillow, it's naptime.)

Why? Because if the story were good, they wouldn't need these tricks.

I am a *Spider-Man 2* fan. Didn't like *1* all that much, loved *2*. Why? Because *2* is a great story. They only introduced one bit of mumbo-jumbo — the accident that turns Dr. Otto Octavius (Alfred Molinayay!) into Dr. Octopus. And thereafter they concentrated on what it's about: the conflict Peter Parker wrestles with about whether or not to be a superhero — the essence of what the Superhero genre is all about. But apparently that was not enough for *S-M 3*. No less than four bits of magic (Quadruple Mumbo Jumbo — for those who have read my book) are employed in the film, including a random meteor that just happens to cross Tobey Maguire's path and turn him "evil." What's missing when we do this is: story. More stories doesn't mean a better movie.

By coincidence I was teaching a FANTASTIC workshop this weekend with 9 writers who all have great, saleable movie ideas. One problem several of them had was the tendency to not stick to their story. What they replaced it with was: more stories. We get insecure that our tale isn't enough sometimes and we tend to "fix it" by running away from it and building up B, C, D, and E stories, and adding more characters — all with fascinating characteristics — and all off the topic! Tell one story well, I keep insisting. And ironically this weekend, we coined a term for veering from the main line of the story: we called it "spidering."

When they put *S-M 4* out there and start advertising that it stars "Academy Award® winner Anthony Hopkins," watch out!

IN THE AIR
May 21, 2009

Last fall something remarkable happened here in the Greater 310 (area code).

In the same week, four top screenwriters went out with pitches they had come up with independently — and guess what?

Four pitches: All the exact same idea.

I won't reveal the pitch. But know that two versions sold, to two different studios.

Yet the "poster" and premise were identical for all four writers.

This phenomenon is not unique. In *Save the Cat!*® I tell of my saga of co-writing a script titled *Really Mean Girls*, but not quick enough to beat *Mean Girls* from getting bought and greenlit first. In that case, the topic was based on an article in the *N.Y. Times* that thousands of people read, and a concept fostered by a great book, *Queen Bees and Wannabes* by Rosalind Wiseman, identifying the "mean girl" phenomenon.

And all *that* example proves is I should have been a faster typer.

Whenever I come up with a movie idea that someone scoops me on, instead of getting mad (or taking pride in my "golden gut"), I say: it was something "in the air." Except in the case that occurred this fall, no such article, trend, or trigger caused the simultaneous eruption on the part of each writer.

It just... happened.

What I'm talking about here isn't about "the business"; it's about the collective unconscious. That's the term C.G. Jung used to describe the deep well of images we know at a subterranean level. And from its depths all kinds of images bubble up with a regularity that make us believe in more than coincidence.

The simultaneous idea phenomenon dovetails with a recent scientific study authored by Christopher C. Davoli and Richard A. Abrams at Washington University in St. Louis that proves for the first time the power of the imagination. In the experiment, subjects were asked to concretize actions they saw in their minds, and it seems to confirm that thoughts are things, and anchored in a more primal benefit.

Titled "Reaching Out With The Imagination," the study hints that capitalizing on what's "in the air" leads to survival. Being better able to bring our imagination to life leads to greater mastery of the world.

But where does the imaginary world leave off and the concrete world begin?

Creativity often leads to pre-cognition, too. I cite the author who wrote about the great ship, the *Titan*, which on its fictional maiden voyage strikes an iceberg (*Iceberg! Iceberg!*) and sinks — except it was written in 1895, long before plans were on the drawing board for the real ship of the almost same name. My other favorite example is the English crossword puzzle writer who in June 1944 got a visit from British Intelligence wondering how his latest puzzle used all the code words for the secret, and yet to unfold, Normandy invasion. But those word clues: Utah, Gold, Sword, and Juno were just a coincidence.

Right?

Being the creative people that we are, we are more in touch with our subconscious than most — or at least more interested in actively trying to tap into it. But what are we tapping in to? Food for thought or thought for food, our mission may be greater than just telling stories, it may be our role in reporting from the front lines of a powerful source of turning the imaginary into the real.

TAPPERS AND LISTENERS
December 31, 2007

I got a little break this Christmas to read some books not necessarily associated with screenwriting.

And yet pretty much everything sends me back to the study of story!

One such example comes from a great book I thoroughly enjoyed and recommend called *Made to Stick* by Chip Heath & Dan Heath.

The basic premise of the book is: Why do some ideas "stick" and others don't? Why, for instance, do urban legends — such as the friend that goes into a strange bar and wakes up in a bathtub with his kidney missing — continue to get passed around virally, while other stories and ideas are DOA.

What grabs us and why is a science that is forever fascinating.

A favorite example from the book — and one that has stuck with *me* — is a social experiment the authors refer to called "Tappers and Listeners." This is one where two people are assigned the task of trying to communicate a simple tune using only tapping to do so. One person, the Tapper, has a song in his head such as "The Star Spangled Banner" but is only allowed to tap the beats of the song to a Listener who must guess the song the poor Tapper is trying to communicate.

The success rate is surprisingly low.

And the funny part is how upset the Tappers get when the experiment fails. "It's the 'Star Spangled Banner,'" they yell. "Aren't you hearing it?"

As screenwriters we are very often the "Tappers." We see our stories! We get it! We understand why our scripts are great! And we get frustrated when others don't.

Why?

Because our movie is playing so clearly in our heads, we can practically taste the popcorn as we sit in the theater and watch our flick unfold.

Why can't everyone else?

To me, this is the essence of what the *Save the Cat!* method helps overcome. Whether it's pitching your idea to strangers at Starbucks, putting up your structure on a virtual board for all to see, or working in one of our many *Cat!* writing groups around the world, we get you out of your isolation and force you to tell us why your movie is great.

But it's all about the simple dilemma of you having a tune in your head and needing to communicate it in a way we understand.

Just for fun try the "Tappers and Listeners" experiment and see for yourself.

And pick up *Made to Stick*, a really nice thought-starter as we head into your best year ever!

2008 is the year you will dazzle us! It's the year you become what you were always meant to be.

It's the year we will hear you loud and clear!

WHY EVAN FAILED
June 28, 2007

I really like Tom Shadyac's *Evan Almighty*. No one else did. Maybe I was just in a good mood when I saw it, and maybe I just like the overall message of the movie.

But wow, what terrible reviews! And the box office was off, too. *Evan* made only $31 million in its first weekend, compared to the $60 million of its "prequel," *Bruce Almighty*'s opening, and the Steve vs. Jim arguments began right away.

But we must ask what went wrong story-wise. Where did the film-makers go off the tracks? Was this sequel just misguided from the start, or was there some other reason this ark was left high and dry?

Why *Evan* came up short while its cousin *Bruce Almighty* succeeded is simple: It's fun to have the powers of God, but no fun to be under God's thumb cursed by having to build an ark.

Also there is a "Watch out for that glacier" problem. As *Deep Impact* and *Armageddon* show, waiting for the inevitable flood — or a comet hitting the earth — means there's a lot of time to kill until that cata-clysmic ending we're all on pins and needles hoping to see!

In short, while *Evan* has a Fun and Games section (all movies do), the "fun" of this particular premise isn't very.

And in hindsight, this simple difference may have decided *Evan's* fate. *Bruce* is more of an "empowerment" tale, *Evan* more a "come-uppance" tale. And apparently in and amongst all the summer movie traffic, fun is always more fun.

Could it be that this simple story problem made all the difference?

I think so.

I have been pitched numerous scripts in the past few years that fall into this same trap. What is "fun" about this comedy? — or any movie we are working on — is something we should all ask our-selves. What is the "empowerment" of your movie notion? Why does the "promise of your premise" sound inviting and an escape, and not a chore?

Our number one job, and the reason I always send writers back to do heavy work on their logline is: We must create a concept that (no matter what the stars or the budget or the studio) people want to RUN to see. It can't just be "cute" or "okay" or "pleasant"; it must grab us by the lapels and drag us to the Cineplex.

On my current list is *Ratatouille*, an original concept that promises great character work, a great message, and the talents of Brad Bird (*The Incredibles*).

It sounds like fun.

Is your concept?

If not, don't write it.

CHAPTER 2

Blake's Blog /May 21, 2007
"If your movie isn't 'about' something, why write it?"

THEMES

THE THEME STATED/B STORY AXIS OF MEANINGFULNESS
May 21, 2007

One of the key breakthroughs I'm having is seeing the importance of Theme Stated — and how the discussion of the theme is found in the B Story.

I am discovering how fascinating the science of story can be.

Take *The Black Stallion*, for instance — a great "boy and his dog" tale. This is one about a boy and his steed. The "Theme Stated" is right there in Minute 7 when the boy's father (Hoyt Axton) tells him the story of how Alexander tamed the wild horse, Bucepholus. "If you can ride that horse, you can have that horse," he says as he repeats the tale. It's what *The Black Stallion* is "about" — not taming a horse per se, but doing the impossible, and taking on the challenge of life in general.

Who is the B Story? Mickey Rooney, the old jockey who's retired from racing and from life. He will take the boy the rest of the way on his quest, and their relationship is all about the theme. It's where it is discussed, and why — by movie's end — when the boy and his horse cross the finish line of the big race, we know the race is about more than that.

It's about doing the impossible.

Theme Stated/B Story must be addressed in your story. If your movie isn't "about" something, why write it? And when you find out what it's about, say it, right up front, then use the B Story to talk about it. The B Story is the "helper" story, and helps the heroes of the A tale transform.

THEMES THAT RESONATE... WITH OSCAR® NOMINEES
January 24, 2008

The nominations for this year's Academy Awards® for screenwriting have been announced and it's an encouraging list.

Encouraging.

Well, sure. Several of the nominations are for writers I am really rooting for, including Diablo Cody, the creative force behind *Juno*, and *Lars and the Real Girl* writer, Nancy Oliver. These two scripts are exactly the types we can be writing. Both are clever ideas, smartly conceived and well executed — and each a spot-on example of how the BS2 works every time.

But these two films also show how it's not enough to have just an original idea and a well-structured story, it must also, as I say in *Save the Cat!*®, be "about something."

And that means theme.

The theme of *Juno* involves the Rites of Passage its heroine undergoes, and her connection to the B Story — the hip Yuppie hubbie, played by Jason Bateman, and his more-than-meets-the-eye wife, Jennifer Garner — is where that character change is discussed. Likewise, the Rites of Passage the titular Lars goes through in *Lars and the Real Girl*, one of mourning, is seen in his relationship with the "real" girl of that film — but who is that?

Theme is directly tied to the B Story of most films; it is the "helper story" and is the subterranean undercurrent of why we appreciate the movie overall, whether we are consciously aware of it during our first viewing or not.

By getting at the heart of why these films work, we can find the meaning in our own — no matter what type we are writing.

THE MOMENT OF CLARITY

I was listening to a speaker talk to a group of us the other night and 45 minutes into it, I was looking for the door.

The subject was the speaker's life and I have to tell ya, it wasn't grabbin' me.

Incident after incident was unveiled, stories about the speaker as a teen, adult, and married man seemed to be of the had-to-be-there variety. And then, magically, he came to a story that tied it all together. It was a simple moment in which he realized what his life had meant. And I got it! Suddenly all the stories added up to something much more.

And my first thought was: I've got to tell my fellow screenwriters about this!

The "this" I mean is what we'll call the **Moment of Clarity**. It's that part of every story — whether it's found in a speech, big budget Hollywood movie, or 30-second commercial for furniture wax — when the hero realizes what the journey has been about. It is the life-changing Huzzah! of the light bulb going on. And understanding the importance of that moment is the secret weapon of anyone who writes *Fade In*.

A recent Moment of Clarity for me came while writing my new book, *Save the Cat!® Goes to the Movies: The Screenwriters Guide to Every Story Ever Told*. In it, I dissect 50 movies to see what makes them tick. At the outset, I thought I knew the importance of that part of the journey where the hero realizes the meaning of it. But it wasn't until I tried to pinpoint the mechanics of how this is executed that I got it. The book has 50 examples seen in films from the 1970s up to their 21st Century counterparts.

And the Moment of Clarity is found in every one.

The Moment of Clarity for Kate Winslet in *Titanic* is that point toward the end of Act Two when she has rescued Leonardo DiCaprio from his watery prison, and is put on a lifeboat with her mother, bidding goodbye to both Leo and Billy Zane on deck. It's a crucial scene. Kate's old life with her mother, trapped by marriage to Billy, has been given back to her. But looking at her mother, Billy, and Leo, Kate realizes she can't go back. She's come too far, and learned too much for having met the love of her life. So Kate makes the only decision anyone can who's seen the error of her ways; she jumps back on the sinking ship to rejoin Leo. Come hell or high water (sorry), she's changed.

Silly comedies have this moment too. One of the silliest is *Planes, Trains and Automobiles*. Busy marketing man Steve Martin is re-routed to Wichita and gets stuck with lovable boor John Candy. John will be Steve's guide in more than getting back to Chicago. For this journey's real lesson is how Steve has been neglecting his family; he's been too involved with his snappy fedora, lush shoes, and the client to realize he's been missing the best part of life. And the guy who'll teach him this lesson is John, who keeps a picture of his wife by his bed every night. Steve's Moment of Clarity comes when, happily riding home on the train after dropping John off, he recalls the trip, and suddenly puts it all together: John has no wife; she's dead. Steve even proves he's changed by doing something he'd never do at the start of this adventure: go back to rescue his pal. It's why the meeting of John and Steve's wife on the doorstep of Steve's home has such lovely resonance: John has brought Steve home as much as Steve has brought John.

The Theme Stated beat gives a movie the reason it matters. (*Planes, Trains and Automobiles* 1987)

You may not realize it watching these movies once or twice or even more, but in both films we are set up for the Moment of Clarity by stating the theme loud and clear. The **Theme Stated** moment of a movie is vital; it's what your movie is about.

In *Titanic*, the Theme Stated moment comes when Leo DiCaprio toasts the rich folk he's been invited to dine with, including the admiring Kate, with: "Make each day count." Whether Kate has this aphorism ringing in her ears while she sits on the lifeboat next to her mother, it's what she's learned — and why she jumps back on the sinking ship. One day, even a last day, with Leo is worth a thousand days of a lifeless future.

Given the lesson of her journey, can she make any other choice?

In the John Hughes classic, the Theme Stated beat is right up front. And like many Theme Stated moments, it's spoken to the hero by someone the hero doesn't think has anything to tell him — and seems unimportant at the time. It's in Minute 12 of this movie when, after phoning his wife about his flight delay, a dejected Steve hears a bit of wisdom from stately, plump John Candy: "I have a motto," he tells Steve. "Like your work. Love your wife." Steve scoffs. He has no idea that's what this trip will be about.

Not yet.

The Theme Stated must also tie into the B Story, or what I like to call the Helper Story, because it *helps* the hero understand the change he needs to make. And it's amazing to understand how Theme Stated is linked to the B Story and how the B Story will link to the hero's final revelation.

In *What Women Want*, starring Mel Gibson as a chauvinistic ad guy who magically hears what women are thinking, the Theme Stated moment occurs at Minute 13. Mel's advertising agency boss, Alan Alda, calls Mel into his office and tells him: "If we don't evolve and grow beyond our natural ability, we're gonna go down." We think Alan's talking about the agency business, but in fact he's talking about Mel. And who will Mel be helped by? None other than the B Story – Helen Hunt. Helen will be the love story and a good example of how the hero learns his lesson in pillow talk with the love interest. Helen will be the one who helps Mel evolve and pushes him toward his final transformation, the Moment of Clarity when he realizes he'd rather be the man Helen admires than get the promotion he thought he wanted when the movie began.

The Moment of Clarity has been set up in all these stories by the Theme Stated-B Story (Helper Story) – Final Transformation link. That is the internal story we need as an audience and must use as screenwriters. As a reminder of how to link up your Moment of Clarity to the mechanics of a well-executed screenplay, here's an easy 1-2-3 to make sure:

1. **State it up front**. The Theme Stated in most movies is just that. I vote we say it early. I like mine by page 5 of a pert and perky 110-page script. And while you may not know it on the first pass, by the time you turn your script in, you should.

2. **Tie the Theme Stated to the B Story**. The B Story is the Helper Story and many times the Love Story. It's the part of the tale that helps the hero internally figure out the meaning of the external story, the action that is the main plot.

3. **Seal the deal!** Sum up what this trip has been about with a definitive Moment of Clarity that shows your hero has not only transformed — but realizes he has.

The Moment of Clarity is the most important part of any story. Why? Because the reason we tell stories is to experience being touched by something divine, that unseen force that makes us realize life is worth living. New knowledge of ourselves or our lives, gratitude for the lives we've had, acceptance of change, love, and the death of old ways of thinking, are divine. It's what lifts us up as an audience. And as writers, reminds us why we do this job. Seeking meaning in the tales we tell allows us to be touched by something special too.

THE TOUCHSTONE SCENE
April 6, 2009

I love our *Save the Cat!* weekends. We have two: the Beats Weekend where we break out your movie, play, or novel idea into the 15 beats of the Blake Snyder Beat Sheet, and the Board Weekend where we start with those 15 and bust them out into the 40 key scenes found in the average story.

In both classes, there is a moment when we find the "touchstone scene'" of your story, which is a key discovery in the development of any script or novel. This is the scene that is most often part of the "Fun and Games" section, and describes what this movie is at core. In *Lethal Weapon*, it's that scene where suicidal Mel Gibson rescues a suicidal man on top of a building by grabbing him and jumping, while his new partner, Danny Glover, watches helplessly from below. In *Black Stallion*, it's the "courtship scenes" between the boy and Black on the desert island, in particular the moment when the boy sits astride his equine pal and rides through the surf — like Alexander taming the wild horse Bucephalus that is at the movie's thematic heart.

This movie or story you've come up with... what is it? What key scene defines your story not just in theme and tone but in its "poster"? It seems easy once you find this "touchstone scene," but until you do, you are often unclear about what you've got. Finding that key moment when concept embraces characters can be the story paint chip you can go back and test with any new scene you create. Does it match? Is it as good as other scenes?

Whenever I hear that scene in your movie during either weekend, I am eager to point it out. It is a great guide to further ideation — and a fun moment in class. And I'm not alone; your fellow writers are often the ones looking for these moments, too. This small group technique is the best I've found for developing a movie, and it starts with the "what is it?" of a key scene that proves what you have is gold!

WHY 1 AND 3 BEAT 2 AND 4
April 6, 2009

I'm available.

That's all I'm saying.

If anyone wants my input on a movie before going into production, don't be shy... just ask.

I mention this in relation to the latest installment of *Indiana Jones*. The dust has settled. The filmmakers are safely in profit — they have a hit! And *Indy 4* is an entertainment to be proud of. But for screen-writers, looking at all four films in the Bullwhip Quartet, it's also a primer in the difference between good and great.

I propose that the first and the third in the series are the best. What do 1 and 3 have that 2 and 4 have less of? Let's take a quick look at *Raiders of the Lost Ark* (1) and *Indiana Jones and the Last Crusade* (3):

1. Both have clearly stated themes and "stories," not just set pieces. And that is key!

2. Both 1 and 3 hit the points of the BS2 like clockwork; they are structurally solid.

3. Both show how relationships change with the action, and are not just tacked onto the story, and...

4. Both have really bad bad guys (and though it's hard to beat Nazis, there is a point to this!)

In short, these things trump any action or set piece and without these elements, story suffers.

Let me just use the word "flabbergasted." I was *flabbergasted* when I revisited the first *Indiana Jones*, which I did in preparation to see this summer's installment. And right there before the adventure begins, Harrison Ford turns to Denholm Elliot and says "I don't believe in black magic or superstition."

Well, guess what? That's the theme of the movie. That is the "arc" of what happens to Indiana Jones in the course of his first adventure. He goes from a non-believer, a scientist, a guy with a lot of whip-snap smarts but no heart, and slowly piece by piece finds "faith."

The ending in which he alone, like Ulysses tied to the mast to hear the Sirens, is witness to the divine intervention of the Ark of the Covenant is proof that he has changed. And yet all along the way his "helper" characters in the B Story have been trying to convince him. "Don't you see, it's a radio transmitter to talk to God," says fellow archeologist Belloq midway through the adventure. But Indiana, at this point, is unfazed.

I was also delighted when I realized how precisely the first *Indiana Jones* hits the marks of the BS2. It had been a while since I saw it and the joy I felt in seeing its Midpoint "false victory" surprised even me. When Indiana discovers the whereabouts of the Ark, only to find Karen Allen is alive, it's the one-two punch of a classic Mid-point. I'd forgot. "Sex at 60!" I yelled when they kissed. That's the oldtime screenwriter's phrase for when the boy and girl kiss at the first hour. It's the A and B Story cross at page 60, followed quickly by one of the great reverses in movies when Indiana has to tie her back up again, or risk his real rescue effort.

But it's all to the point of the "spine" of the story, the "greatest event that ever happened to Indiana Jones" — the story about how he started without faith and, over the course of a wild adventure, found it, by amending his past misdeeds, learning to love, and dis-covering a power greater than himself!

A movie that's "about something" is also part of *Indiana Jones and the Last Crusade*, the third installment co-starring Sean Connery. Here again, 3 has a story beneath the hijinks, that of a relationship be-tween a father and son, and the son's quest to make his dad proud. Amid all the chase scenes and derring-do and wonderful set pieces, that is how each bit "moves the story forward."

Once again, Indy is learning faith here, too. And structurally, it is also one of the great examples of what I call the "Five Point Finale" in Act Three when Indy has a choice: the prize of a great archeo-logical treasure or saving his father's life. It is one of the great "dig, deep down" moments that ranks right up there with "Use the force, Luke" to show what real faith is.

Finally, let's talk Nazis. It's not a coincidence that they are part of 1 and 3 and absent from 2 and 4. "Make the bad guy badder" is sure-fire screenplay physics that guarantees your hero will be bigger, too. In 2, the evil is vague. In 4, it's vague-er. And there is a blur even in the script that can't quite decide if Communism is bad at all. What are the consequences of the Soviets getting 4's treasure? Hard to judge.

Good as they are, 2 and 4 are missing these elements. Same great character, same great team running the show, same top flight A-list writers, and yet 1 and 3 are stories that are truly memorable. 2 and 4, less so.

So take note. Your script too must be "about something" and have meaning that touches us at a primal, and even spiritual level.

Do so, and *your* story will be memorable, too.

HEALTHY, VIBRANT, NO LIMITS
July 21, 2008

My theory is we're just creating and marketing our stories better than ever before. The intersection of art and commerce is widening to include more of us, and whether we are veterans with movies already in the works, or fresh-faced aspirants striving for our first brass ring, there are more chances for success than we can gather into one bushel basket.

While the cineplexes loaded up with ticket buyers this weekend, I got to speak to a really generous and receptive audience of writers at the Pacific Northwest Writers Association. The PNWA is mostly about books — fiction and non-fiction — but one of the theories sweeping the weekend conference was how screenplay structure can inform any kind of writing. And when it comes to codifying what that is, I think *Save the Cat!* explains the movie template more easily than any other method.

I spoke for 90 minutes and yes, my new suit was a hit! But what I really loved were the questions from writers — what a smart group! By the time we were finished, I felt that I'd made a few hundred new friends — and hopefully new converts to this common-sense structure.

What's it all about?

Communication.

Tell me your story.

But bring me into your world as if I don't know anything about what's on your mind — because I don't.

Have compassion for me, your potential ticket buyer or reader, who really wants to give you the benefit of the doubt, but will only give you my attention as long as you intrigue me with a grabber of a headline, a hero, or theory I can identify with — and a progression of ideas that lead me from one stop to the next in solving "the problem" you told me about up front.

How do my old ideas die for having come along with you, and how have you replaced the old with something truly new, and a little bit divine? Every story, essay, or argument must have that spark, that life-giving and mysterious bolt of lightning that renews my faith — and leads me to something I never dreamed possible.

There is no ceiling on the number of movie theaters we can pack with ticket buyers, and no boundaries on our creativity, whether we are movie writers or novelists, short story tellers or essayists supreme. If you can communicate, your horizons will have to be raised and readied with greater expectations.

There are no limits — and no time like the present — to expand our skills and enlarge our tents!

THE CHECKLIST
July 7, 2008

Is there a checklist we can reference to see what makes a successful story?

That is the assumption I am operating under, and in the development process I follow with the writers I work with, in and out of the studio system, it proves time and again to be not only real — but effective.

It starts with concept. Is it understandable? Does it "grab" me? Or are we going to have to rely on other factors such as casting, special effects, budget, or "an act of God" to pull it off? No gimmicks, please. No one-joke premises expanded to the breaking point. It can be simple, sure. But simple in a way that promises depth when explored. A richness, a primal-ness, that just speaking the words of your idea — excites me!

If satisfying enough to attempt, can the concept be exploited to its very maximum, can we draw from it the excitement, freshness, "trailer moments" — as well as Moments of Clarity — that make a story sing?

If we can say, "Check!" or "Okay, what's next?" then we move on. We start to "beat this sucker out" and when we do, can we find HUGE change in the protags? Why is this "the most important adventure that ever happened to the hero of this movie"? One way to judge is to check out if the beginning and the end are opposites; is the "snapshot of the world before" this adventure begins and the "snapshot of the world after" so different, so breathtakingly bi-polar that we know for sure we've been somewhere? And know we'll never be the same?

Okay. Check. Move on.

Do Acts 1, 2, and 3 each exploit the essence of what those three worlds demand? Is "Thesis" ripe with problems? Not just idiosyncratic problems for our hero, but systemic ones for the world he lives in? Is the "upside-down version of the world" in "Anti-thesis" so amazingly new and otherworldly that we cannot believe this hero will survive? And once he does "die" on page 75, is there a "Synthesis" in Act Three in which what he was, and what he has learned, combine to create a "Third Way" that is the lesson of the movie?

Check?

Finally: theme. What is this "about"? What is the moral of the story? And more important, did we have a brush with the divine? This, to me, is what it really comes down to. Did we see a "supernatural power" at work in this story that lifts it — and us — beyond our ordinary selves, and gives us cavemen a new way to look at the world in an inspired way? It doesn't have to be "Use the force, Luke!"; it can be the divine of a friendship unearned yet granted to us anyway, a last minute reprieve before the sentence we deserve is carried out, or a simple kiss from the girl we never expected to have faith in us, who bestows the courage we need to be what we did not think possible. It's looking into the black maw of nothingness and finding...

That's all I'm asking for at the movies — something extraordinary. And yes, that "lightning in a bottle" is hard to capture, even harder to describe. But if we build it, they will come. If we check our checklist, and know at least that we are looking for it, and demand it's in there, then every silly comedy, big action adventure, deep Oscar*-nominated triumph, and seemingly simple love story will knock our socks off.

Different stories.

Same checklist.

What's yours?

ONE STORY
March 17, 2008

I had the opportunity to speak to an amazing group of creative professionals on Friday. I have a lot of good friends among this group and felt very welcome, but this was different. Something special happened, and I've been walking on Cloud 9 ever since.

In my one-hour talk I focused on *Save the Cat!* *Goes to the Movies* and the 10 unique genres I feel break open the discussion of story in a new way. Just like the BS2 and its useful "handles" like "Fun and

Games" and "All Is Lost," having these 10 genres lets us reference story by type, so when you say "Oh, it's mostly Golden Fleece with a little Buddy Love," I know exactly what you mean.

But ultimately, what really hit home for me on Friday is there really is only one story: the story of something amazing!

The more I work at this, the more I see how no matter what genre we're working in, every story is about being touched by the divine. The difference between just an entertaining movie and a great one is finding that place in it when the hero realizes he's changed for the experience, that he gave up something he thought was true and found lacking, only to find faith in something beyond himself that he needed to take that last step to triumph. Love, friendship, gratitude, and yes, the death of old ideas, are divine and can change us, and change our lives.

I joked with the audience that I find these moments everywhere, even in unlikely places. While watching *Galaxy Quest* the other night, I was struck by Alan Rickman's character. He plays a Shakespearean actor doomed to portray a Mr. Spock-ish icon on a *Star Trek*-like series and has a corny line he is known for — and hates saying. It isn't until the end when an admiring alien dies in his arms that he says the line again, his performance suddenly not a performance, the line suddenly flooded with meaning. It catches us off guard, and fills us with emotion for a simple reason: It isn't what this character expected when he woke up that morning; he didn't know he'd find meaning in the mundane, but he did. And the experience transforms him, and us.

I need a miracle every day. As a human being I just want to know it's worth going on. Tell me one story, again and again, I don't care how many times, that lets me know it's worth it.

As writers our mission is to tap into that deeper source and put it right into our stories, no matter how silly, or how epic, or how intellectual a story we think we're telling.

CHAPTER 3

Save the Cat!® /p.63
*"The logline is your story's code, its DNA,
the one constant that has to be true."*

TITLES & LOGLINES

WHAT MAKES A GREAT LOGLINE?
March 8, 2006

I am starting to see a lot more spec sales in the trades!!

This makes me very happy.

Maybe… FINALLY… Hollywood is looking outside the studio gates for their movie ideas. 'bout time!

One recent sale I cited in my seminar last weekend was one that proved the good loglines are ones where I hit my forehead and say: *Dooohh!*

Why didn't *I* think of that?

Two first-time writers sold their spec to Paramount. Title: *Identity Crisis*. Concept: A groom wakes up on his wedding day with amnesia and must piece together the events of his bachelor party from the night before.

It's simple. It's primal (weddings are). It doesn't sound expensive. And it's targeted at the sweet spot of the marketplace: youth.

Come to think of it: I HAVE pitched this idea!!! But that's okay. We live. We learn. We move on.

It's beneficial to compare the ideas that sold with your own loglines to see if you too have the four elements that make for a successful one. Most of those that sell do. And it's a good thing to keep reading loglines; the rhythm of what makes a good one becomes more obvious as you read one after the next.

Identity Crisis doesn't take many words to describe. The logline is evocative of a whole movie (the concept blooms in my mind when I hear it) and it has a target and the cost of the movie implied in the idea.

And while *Identity Crisis* isn't the world's greatest title, it at least "Says What It Is" — which is the key to any good title.

Go forth and do likewise.

TITLE BLUR
September 10, 2007

I heard an interesting anecdote this weekend.

A couple wanted to go see the new "Western" they had heard so much about.

So when they got up to the ticket window at the Octoplex and scanned the list of movies playing, they bought two tickets for what they assumed was just that.

And off they went to see *Shoot 'Em Up*.

I hear they were disappointed — and not just because they didn't see a Western. *Shoot 'em Up* turns out to be a wild urban gangsta flick. Imagine this couple's reaction when they realized what had happened.

Apparently they missed the *3:10 to Yuma*, and I'm not surprised. You know and I know that this is based on the Elmore Leonard novel and the 1957 cowboy saga starring Glenn Ford and Van Heflin, but not everyone does. See! Not even making a remake guarantees ticket buyers will know about it enough to see the film. Or even understand what genre it is based on its title.

This speaks to what I talk about in my books — man, I love saying that! — and that is the importance of making your title and logline first and foremost comprehensible.

What is the logline of your movie? What is the title? Does the title "say what it is" in a way that is unique, compelling — and clear?

If not, make it so.

But this title blur also applies to other areas. If you have a business or a new product or are seeking a job and writing your resume, try to ask yourself what your title and logline is in these cases, too.

Is the logline on your new product — and what it does — clear? Is the "What is it?" about what you offer a potential employer easy to explain and deliver on a primal level?

Good marketing men know about this problem whether it's a movie, a person, or a product!

I find this topic fascinating, and in a world of a million entertainment choices, it's vital for us screenwriters to understand.

Take toothpaste, for example. Crest fights cavities. Ultra Brite whitens teeth. Aqua Fresh tastes good. Millions of dollars are spent each year to reinforce these simple concepts. Each has a primal punch, too. Crest: safety, health. Ultra Brite: appeal to the opposite sex. Aqua Fresh: my kids will brush their teeth if they like the taste.

To me, this is the essence of good communication generally. A clear idea about something of primal interest — isn't that what it's all about?

And it starts with a "title and logline" we communicate well, and takes into account the busy lives of consumers who don't have more than a minute to make a choice — be it what movie to watch or what toothpaste to use.

Avoid title blur.

Be clear! Communicate well! Excite! Invite!

From concept to execution, every step of the way, this is our job as storytellers in the market place of ideas!

TITLE, TITLE, WHO'S GOT THE TITLE?
May 28, 2009

What's the most important single feature of a great screenplay?

All of it!

No part of a script is any more important than any other, nor will a single "silver bullet" save the day.

My favorite saying of late is that a winning story isn't just one great idea, but a thousand.

Concept. Logline. The transformation of the hero. The Midpoint crunch. The "lightbulb" above the head of the hero that makes him resist the horrible truth in the Bad Guys Close In section. The All Is Lost when that horrible truth is revealed! The Finale in which we learn if the hero can pass "The Final Exam" — or not.

All of it: vital.

But dudes, and dudettes, I give you: Title.

Because a good one is gold and a bad one is not.

A good title must "say what it is!" and yet give us a fresh, intriguing invitation to your party that gives us a hint of the type and tone of the festivities we're about to attend. And that's some tight writing right there.

Our hero's lightbulb moment.

Indeed, evidence abounds in the cutthroat world of moviedom, that if we don't win the audience's interest in our story from that first set of words, often success slips from our grasp.

Some cautionary title tales of late: *State of Play* starring Russell Crowe. I saw the movie. Enjoyed it. Lots of fun. But even after seeing the film I still don't know what the title refers to, and that had a lot to do with its poor showing. This follows another Russell Crowe film, co-starring Leonardo DiCaprio and directed by my favorite director of all time, Ridley Scott. It was an even greater story, and yet here too, no one went. Why? In my opinion it's because for all the lure of its star power and importance of the topic, I didn't know what it was about, and its title, *Body of Lies*, is one of those generic ones, like the infamous *For Love or Money*.

It told me nothing.

I hate to say it, but if your story is special, it should have a special name, and deferring to placeholder titles (even if they're based on a book or series of the same name) is a hint to an audience that it may not be special. And I'll tell you something else: The lack of a good title may be indicative of confusion on your part about "what it is." If you can't name it, if your headline doesn't flow right into the story, there may be trouble with it.

If this sounds like *your* story: Take note.

All of the above is proof of the power of the writer. Big stars will not necessarily open a movie. Millions of dollars thrown at an advertising campaign will not either. We, the audience, must be drawn in by a great story idea that's fresh, and primal, and a title that not only "says what it is" but does so in a way that grabs us.

Before you settle for those titles that are "less than," if your story is about redemption and so you call it... *Redemption*, take a breath. Try something new. Find a title that "says what it is" but with a twist.

And we will run to your movie, not walk.

4 X 4 X 4
May 5, 2008

The past Sunday's *L.A. Times* had a special section devoted to all the movies that are coming to theaters in the next three months, and a list of sure-fire loglines that go with them! It's a great preview of what we can expect and a really great job by the *Times*.

Anytime I read a good logline, I start to think of my own pitches and my own movies I'm creating.

And I get excited!

I want to play, too! That's the thought that comes to mind when I see what other movies are on tap. (I have this same reaction at the Coming Attractions — the best part of going to the movies.) It revs my creative engines thinking of how I can concoct a logline as good or better than what's "Coming Soon."

Like the loglines I read in the *Times* this Sunday, those that grab me follow the rules we discuss in *Save the Cat!*. Funny, but it works every time!

The basic components that must be included in a successful logline are:

— A type of protagonist (meaning *adjective*-hero)

— A type of antagonist (meaning *adjective*-opposing force)

— A conflict (and it better be sparking!) and

— An open-ended question (what will happen?)

I also added further spice to this basic need by requesting four more components:

— A sense of irony (that's what a "hook" really is)

— A compelling mental image (I always say that "A good movie pitch is like dropping a flare into a diamond mine; when you say it, my mind bursts with ideas, drama, and images that dazzle)

— Audience and cost (Who is this for? Does it make economic sense?)

— A killer title! (Please don't pitch anything called *Redemption* or *For Love or Money!*)

We're in the shank of the Golden Age of creativity at the movies! Be it a summer tentpole movie, quirky Indie, or homemade doc, there are more opportunities out there for us now than ever before.

Let's play, too!

OF BUMPER MUSIC, WORD PLAY, AND MOVIE TITLES
April 17, 2008

One of my favorite early morning rituals is waking up, making coffee, and listening to KFI-AM's "Handel on the News," a local radio staple here in Los Angeles. From 6:00-7:00 each morning, the irrepressible host and his crew give a humorous take on the headlines as we bleary-eyed early risers come to. Their raucous and un-PC jokes are jaw-dropping so early every morning. But what I really tune in for is the musical lead-ins to each news story. Why? Because the musical bumpers and bridges are witty counterpoint in itself.

A story about a priest abuse case is led into with Connie Francis singing "Where the Boys Are" and any item about Governor Schwarzenegger inevitably is trumpeted by "Springtime for Hitler" from *The Producers*.

It reminds me of the way Paul Schaeffer on David Letterman's show can be scathingly funny in his walk-on music for guests. And in some cases, like the toreador march that still introduces comedian Don Rickles, it is a signature song that perfectly "says what it is" — Rickles is the matador, you are the bull.

The guy who used to have the job of picking these musical bullets on "Handel on the News" retired last month and the tryouts to replace him have been tough to listen to. Not everyone has the musical knowledge to pull from, plus the wit to be thoughtful and not ham-handed in their choices. It's tempting to use "Leaving on a Jet Plane" for a story about airport delays, but not as funny as "Anticipation."

The skill is in picking musical bumpers that don't hit you over the head, but make you laugh as you realize "That was witty!"

I bring this up, believe it or not, as a means of discussing something screenwriters ask me about all the time, namely, how to come up with a title for your movie! Because word play is what it's all about.

In my book, *Save the Cat!*, I talk about the importance of the title, and how a good one can increase your odds of success. I note that a good title isn't blunt or "on the nose," meaning if you have a movie that is about redemption, don't call it *Redemption*. There is also the vague title, like 2005's *The Island* which, I'm convinced, hurt ticket sales. (Are there castaways? Is Dr. Moreau involved?) And the curse of being too general in your title leads to my least favorite title of all time, *For Love or Money*, which has been used three times in movie history and I can't tell you the story of any version. It's so general, you could use it for any movie: *Gone with the Wind* = *For Love or Money*, *The Godfather* = *For Love or Money*.

See what I mean?

In my career, my favorite titles that I've come up with have been just... "off the nose." Colby Carr and I found a great one for our "plumb and plumber" comedy, *Drips*, that we sold to Disney. I sometimes have even started with the title and built the story to match as we did with *Nuclear Family* that sold to Amblin. Like a good movie idea, often there is no rhyme or reason for how we know we got one! We just know.

CHAPTER 4

Save the Cat! ® /p. 21
"Give me the same thing ... only different!"

GENRES

CAT! 2 – A WINNER IN EVERY WAY
December 6, 2007

Just heard from my publisher and it's official — *Save the Cat!*® *Goes to the Movies* is the fastest-selling new title in the *20* year history of the company!

When the idea to write a sequel to the first *Save the Cat!*® was broached, it being the "Last Book on Screenwriting You'll Ever Need," (ha!) I was hesitant. But I'm so glad I answered the *Cat!*-call, and took the challenge! It was a lot of work, but reviewing over 200 movies to get the 50 that I write about in the book was an amazing experience!

To me, the 10 unique genres I discuss in the new book, from "Monster in the House" to "Fool Triumphant" to "Superhero," redefine what we look for in our storytelling process. What is the essence that makes a scary movie scary? What are we REALLY looking for when we throw an "ordinary guy" into an "extraordinary circumstance" — as found in most "Dude with a Problem" movies? What is it about a "Buddy Love" tale, be it a rom-com or a "boy and his dog" story, that makes us shiver with longing?

By dissecting stories in this brand new way, we are better writers! And even if we're just movie fans, taking a new look at our favorite films, and figuring out what makes them work, is empowering knowledge!

The chapter I am proudest of is that covering movies deemed "Institutionalized." These are stories about "groups" and whether or not we should join them. The name of this genre speaks to the underlying question: Who's crazier — them or me? And this is a long-standing, and very primal, dilemma. As cavemen we like to belong. We might even find logic in "tradition" and "rules" that keep us safe. But what about that inner voice that says: Hold on, wait a minute, maybe what the group is asking me to do is *wrong*?! It's the beginning of a great dramatic conflict.

It may also have something to do with the fact these are films I love.

How to use this book is hopefully clear but after fielding a number of emails from writers asking me just that, I'd say *Save the Cat!* *Goes to the Movies* is most useful in figuring out how to write the story type *you* love. I think I drop about a million hints in the book that the prime directive of audiences is: "Give me the same thing only different." So when you look at the arc of the movies I break down in the book, the obvious question is: How are you going to keep the building blocks of the story type — and still extend and enhance the line?

The stories we like to hear go back to the Bible. And I cite many stories that are the antecedents of those we see at the Multiplex. We like to hear the same ones for a reason — we are human beings who find ourselves in the exact same circumstances as our ancestors, who wonder whether or not it's worth it to get up every day and hit it one more time. These stories tell us that it is. And whether it's a wild magical journey like *Eternal Sunshine of the Spotless Mind* or classic studio fare like *Gladiator* or *Alien*, the message is the same.

We are just keepers of this generation's versions of the stories we've been telling forever. Our job is to find the new twists, the new tones, and the exciting new story elements that make these stories speak to us... then pass them on to the next generation.

What a *freekin'* cool job we have — and what a wonderful responsibility.

The more we learn about the essence of whatever story we're telling, the more likely we are to succeed! And taking that task seriously is what makes us winners!

And yes, there will be a *Save the Cat!* 3.

LITTLE MISS SUNSHINE – A GOLDEN FLEECE
August 2, 2006

Went to the movies last weekend. I really have not been seeing enough. I used to regularly have "Movie Day" when I would buy four tickets at the cineplex and see four movies in an afternoon — even if I didn't stay for the whole performance, I had an idea of what each was about.

No longer. And dang! I miss it. You would be appalled at the movies I have not seen this summer. But I am catching up.

When you see a good one, you know it. And *Little Miss Sunshine* did it for me.

Why? Because in addition to being a type of movie we know, it hits all the beats in the BS2!

Little Miss Sunshine is a Golden Fleece, so defined as "a team that goes on the road to achieve a prize — that turns out not to be what they expect." It comes from the myth of Jason and the Argonauts. Jason sets out to be king, but on the road with his team, including Hercules (the Vin Diesel of his era), he finds much more. Movies like this include *Saving Private Ryan*; *Planes, Trains and Automobiles*; and even sports sagas like *Dodgeball* and heist movies like *Ocean's Eleven*.

LMS is that.

Check it out and see if you agree.

THE GOOD SHEPHERD AND *CASINO ROYALE*: SPY MOVIES?

April 9, 2007

I've been catching up on some movies — just for fun finally! So far, my favorites in the "New Releases" section are *Casino Royale* (Superhero) and *The Good Shepherd* (Institutionalized). The Blockbuster customer will find them both in the Spy Movie aisle, but we *Cat!-tastics* know differently, don't we?

Casino Royale falls into the "Superhero" genre because James Bond (Daniel Craig) has all the qualities of the hero of that category, including a bad guy mirror image I am calling the "Nemesis," who represents "self will" to the superhero's pure ability. All SH heroes are "the chosen one," special beings with special skills, and all variations on the Christ figure sent here to save us. Their curse is that they KNOW they're special — and know they must pay a price for being so. The bad guys in all these movies all have some kind of "plan" or special man-made contraption that will make them special — even though they know deep down they aren't. Look at *The Matrix*, *Gladiator*, and *Casino Royale*; they all have the same good guy/bad guy dynamic! And each of these has a moment in Act Three where the hero dies and is born again! In *Casino Royale*, the bad guy is so focused on making his brain solve his problems that his eye bleeds blood! If only he had what Bond has: faith.

The Good Shepherd really deserves the description of "the Godfather of CIA movies" — fabulous! And like all Institutionalized tales, it's about the pros and cons of joining a group. It is actually more like *Goodfellas* because it is about someone who is brought into the group and shown to change as he experiences it. Stay or go, believe in the group or not, is the ongoing conflict. Very caveman-like! *GS* spans thirty years of CIA history through which "Naif" Matt Damon joins and falls prey to the agency's corruption. Naifs often start out this way in movies of the "I" kind, but end up the hardened veteran (check out *Training Day*, in which Ethan Hawke makes this same trip in a single 24-hour period that takes Matt 30 years to do).

These stories keep repeating! Their elements keep repeating! Why? Because we like to hear them and hear the message they underscore.

MICHAEL CLAYTON, *NETWORK*, *THE GODFATHER*, AND YOU
February 21, 2008

I have been kidding the marketers of Michael Clayton in the liner notes of this blog of late. It's not that they did a poor job getting the word out on George Clooney's fall release, it just points up the problem we all face of how to sell an idea that doesn't fit neatly into a box.

We'll start with that title. I guess they had Julia Roberts' *Erin Brockovich* in mind. That was the name of a person, too, and that worked out okay. Except the real Erin Brockovich was part of the pitch, the true-life story that movie was based on was well known, and the real Erin turned out to be a hell of a spokesperson who wound up with an investigative reporting show of her own. So maybe just a name as the title isn't the best way to "say what it is."

And let's not go into "The Truth Can Be Adjusted," the overlay that accompanied the poster for *Michael Clayton*. What exactly does THAT mean? And, having now seen the movie, I am even more confused about what that has to do with the story.

If only the marketing department at Warner Brothers had read *Save the Cat!® Goes to the Movies*!

That book is all about genre, my theory being that most great stories fall into 10 story types — and each follows patterns that audiences love to see.

We frankly can't get enough of "Monster in the House" flicks, which make up Chapter One of the book. This is any monster movie, usually enhanced by an isolated "house" into which the star is loosed to ply his trade. You can tell this story again and again (as long as yours has a fresh twist) and we will line up to see it. Why? Because if you can recreate the elements of a successful MITH you will have audiences eating out of your monster's thorny little hand.

"Dude with a Problem"? This is the type of movie that pits an "ordinary man" against "extraordinary circumstances" — just take a look at how *North by Northwest* begat *Three Days of the Condor* which begat *The Bourne Supremacy*. See? Even down to core elements, such as the "Eye of the Storm" character in each of those tales (Eva Marie Saint, Faye Dunaway, and Franka Potente, respectively) who appear to assist the "dude on the run," these repeating patterns are vital to success.

As long as you know what elements are important, the template works every time.

It's Michael Clayton vs. the Company in this Institutionalized tale. (*Michael Clayton* 2007)

Michael Clayton may have stumped the marketing department at Warner Brothers, but it didn't stump me — at least once I finally saw it. While they were wrestling (I'm sure) with questions like: Is it a comedy? Is it a thriller? Is it a spiritual drama? To me, the answer is easy. Michael Clayton is a type of movie I call "Institutionalized."

Tales of the "Institutionalized" kind are all about "the group." And we as cavemen GET that dilemma. The "group" takes us Neanderthals on the Woolly Mammoth hunt every year, and every year — thanks to the tradition of how we hunt — half our guys get killed. Only the weenies in the tribe object to this tradition, and those that object too loudly are drummed out of the cave. But YOU know there's a better way. Can you fight your elders to convince them they're wrong? Or do you need to burn the cave down and start again?

That's what *Michael Clayton* is essentially about. Instead of cavemen, it's lawyers. As the titular Michael Clayton, George Clooney is the guy who has gone along with the tribe his whole life. He's been fed, and sheltered, and yes even loved by his tribe. And guess what?

They're wrong.

So what is he going to do?

It's not only a great primal tale... it's the oldest story in our DNA.

If only we had been told that's what the story was, we might have gone to see it!

Further proof that *Michael Clayton* falls into this category comes with more comparison and contrast with other "Institutionalized" stories, and lo! A lot of other interesting coincidences pop up.

Take a look at the "crazy" Tom Wilkenson character in *Michael Clayton*, then look at that very same character played by Peter Finch in another "I" tale: *Network*. "Who's crazier them or me?" is the ongoing question (and one reason I picked the name "Institutionalized" to describe this genre type). In fact, the line "You're crazy!" appears in many tales of the "I" kind — from *MASH* to *Training Day* to *American Beauty*.

Last night while watching *The Godfather* on AMC, I noted how it too so nicely falls into this category. Poor Al Pacino is sucked into his family's business, little knowing until the end of *Godfather 2* that he has committed spiritual "suicide" for the cause. Al's line in *Godfather 3* sums up the "I" dilemma: "Just when I thought I was out, they pull me back in!"

Can we have a more appropriate theme song for this story?

Point of all this is, if YOU are writing a movie like this, or trying to sell it to a public who knows nothing except that "George Clooney is in it," it's always a good idea to figure out what your movie is most like. It helps us as writers figure out why we're writing, and it helps marketers tell us "What is it?"

BLAKE'S TOP TEN
January 16, 2006

Golden Globes tonight and the subject comes up: what are your Top Ten movies of the year?

As a former movie critic I still get the question. But now my interest is in how my favorite movies help you to write yours.

Here are my Top Ten Most Helpful Examples Of Good Movies To Learn From for 2005.

1. *40-Year-Old Virgin*. Why? Degree of difficulty. This "Fool Triumphant" could have been crass and turned out to be sweet — with a GREAT "Pope in the Pool" moment BTW. Ten points to the person who can tell me what that moment is!

2. *Capote*. Beat for beat a textbook example of the BS2 and a classic "Golden Fleece" in which what we think the goal of the journey is, turns out not to be at all. A GREAT "Theme Stated" moment right there in minute 5. Take a look when it comes out on DVD.

3. *Cinderella Man*. Despite the terrible title (why doesn't anyone ever call me about these things?!) a wonderful, deep, and moving example of the "Superhero" genre.

4. *Crash*. Yes, despite its ensemble form, it too has a clear cut BS2 including a great synthesis moment at the end.

5. *Kiss Kiss, Bang Bang*. Must give kudos to Shane Black and at the same time advise everyone else: No breaking of the fourth wall please. When you create a worldwide, billion dollar hit franchise — then we'll talk.

6. *Upside of Anger*. Mike Binder directed this "Rites of Passage" tale and gives us one of the best portraits of alcoholism in main characters Kevin Costner and Joan Allen.

7. *The Constant Gardener*. "Dude With A Problem" indeed. An ordinary man, who likes it that way, is drawn into an extraordinary world by the death of his wife.

8. *Wallace & Gromit: The Curse of the Were-Rabbit*. Surely the best family film of the year.

9. *Wedding Crashers*. A "Buddy Love" and a $200 million hit because we knew going in what it was about just from the poster! Also ties with *40-Year-Old Virgin* for "Best Title."

10. *King Kong*. No, not a "Monster In the House." A love story. And I for one loved the fact they took their time getting there.

So you see, there are examples of winning movies in almost every one of my 10 movie genres. If you are working on a genre that matches one of these films, take a look — and stay tuned for the Golden Globes!

KING KONG: BUDDY LOVE
December 15, 2005

Great movie, *King Kong*. Saw it Monday in a packed theater in Westwood, CA and three hours flew by. But because my mission in life is figuring out how movies work, the big debate on my mind was: Is *King Kong* a "Monster in the House" or a "Buddy Love"??

Evil is let in the door when a sin is committed in a typical MITH movie. Havoc and death reign as a result. *Alien*, *Fatal Attraction*, *The Ring* and *American Psycho* all qualify.

King Kong does not.

For though *King Kong* involves lots of monsters, what it's "about" is the love story between Naomi Watts and Mr. Big and Tall. *Old Yeller*, *E.T.* and even *Rain Man* are more like what this story concerns: the risks and reward of loving someone special, someone the world does not necessarily understand. Many "boy and his dog" tales are like this and Kong is no exception.

Why is this important to us?

As storytellers we must always be asking ourselves: What is our story "about?" And seeing the elements of what makes our story work in the stories others tell helps us figure it out.

CHAPTER 5

Save the Cat! ®/p. 50
*"Give your hero the most conflict, the longest journey,
and the most primal goal."*

HEROES

MORE WAYS TO SAVE THE CAT!
August 4, 2008

Of the principles spelled out in the *Save the Cat!* ® *ouevre*, none is more important than its namesake. "Save the Cat!" is one of many catch phrases we employ for identifying common tricks in storytelling and communication that we inherently sense — and now can put a term to.

The "Save the Cat!" beat in any movie, novel, or story is that moment when we meet its hero and he does something "nice" — like save a cat — that makes us like him and want to root for him.

It is, I'm finding, a ritualistic turning point, a truly magical event when we in the audience "step into the shoes" of, and become, the hero. And because of that, his story now becomes *our* story.

Though it doesn't have to be that bald a moment, it must be considered in any type of communication — in a 30-second commercial, a political ad, a YouTube short, or even a speech one is giving to an audience. And we see textbook examples at the movies all the time!

Will Smith "saves a lion cub" in *I Am Legend*; Steve Carell "pats a dog" in the early moments of the recent *Get Smart*; and Robert Downey Jr. tries to "save his pals" in the beginning of *Ironman*.

The "Save the Cat!" moment is also seen in a 30-second spot for Kentucky Fried Chicken when a harried stay-at-home Dad or Mom, who wants to make a well-balanced meal for the kids — but doesn't have time to cook — comes to the rescue with a family fast food favorite; or when a politician cites good deeds done in the service of others; or when a radio talk show host tells his listeners a self-deferential story that compels those listening to "identify," and thus, stay tuned.

For that very small consideration, we as an audience think: "I'm like that! I'm rooting for him!"

And there are a million more variations on how to do this that aren't so obvious, too.

There is the "Kill the Cat!" moment I point out in *Save the Cat!* Goes to the Movies in regard to Reese Witherspoon's character Elle Woods in Legally Blonde. When Elle learns that her boyfriend, Warner, is not only not going to ask her to marry him ("I want a Jackie and not a Marilyn"), Elle is essentially smooshed. Up till then, Elle is just verging on annoying, put down for being blonde — and kind of deserving the label! But from this moment on, we want Elle to win. Why? Because we too have been "smooshed" in life and readily identify with wanting to get some sense of justice.

Another method is "Save the Cat! by proxy." Often a hero in a film will not be likeable on the surface, but there may be someone in his or her circle whom we do trust, who makes a statement of support. In *What Women Want*, in the introduction of the "ladies man" Mel Gibson plays in that film, there is a sense the narrator can't help liking this lovable rogue, and by proxy so must we!

There is also "Kill the Cat! by proxy" wherein a not so likeable guy is hated by someone who is worse — and that is its own recommendation for liking an "unlikeable" hero. A classic example of this is found in *Pulp Fiction* when we meet John Travolta and Samuel L. Jackson, killers, but made lovable not only by their funny patter, but the fact that there is someone who is worse! Marcellus (Ving Rhames) tossed a fellow hitman off the roof for giving Marcellus' wife a foot massage. In this universe, we now know, there are degrees of badness, and our guys aren't the gold medalists.

Recently, in *The Dark Knight*, I'd argue that the "Save the Cat!" moment comes when we meet Batman, by definition the moodiest and most depressed of superheroes, who is fighting not only criminals, but the citizens of Gotham who hate him and call him a "terrorist." The caped crusader even runs afoul of Batman lookalikes with guns who are true vigilantes. Poor Batman is so under the thumb of others, so misunderstood, so put down and despised, we expect him to throw in the cowl. But he doesn't. He is either a glutton for punishment, or maybe worth pulling for?

Heroes like this are worth following for awhile... if only to learn why they do what they do! The mistake is to not care about this first step in getting any act of communication off the ground. Storytelling is like building a case in court. We start with an audience who knows... nothing. What do we want them to know? What do we need them to know to keep their interest?

All stories are like this: an argument, a debate about a particular theme or "moral to the story." What are we trying to say — and who will be our spokesman? Whether it's a classic hero, anti-hero, non-human hero (*WALL-E*), or even if it's just us — someone making a speech, or the person trying to get across a point of view in a debate or in court — we must be conscious of an audience who isn't standing in our shoes and must be brought along in order for them to do so.

And there is always a new way to skin... or save... a cat!

GOD SAVE THE CAT!

January 29, 2007

A friend called up the other day and said: "There's a 'Save the Cat!' moment in *The Queen*, have you seen it?"

Hadn't.

I did have a screener of the film, however, kindly sent to WGA members as part of the studio's effort to promote its filmmakers for award consideration.

Love those screeners!

So along with some friends we had a Sunday Evening Cinecale — and what a great movie! Helen Mirren as the titular Queen E, and Michael Sheen even better as the newly elected PM, Tony Blair, made for wonderful political combatants. The conflict: the controversy over the death of Princess Diana (an event that marked the first time I'd ever learned of a breaking news story from the Internet). The movie details the outpouring of love for the "People's Princess" that took the Royal family and the government by surprise.

The story is the slow coming to grips with this event by Mirren. The very icy Queen of England, along with consort Phillip (James Cromwell) and the rest of the Royals, are portrayed as chilly in their initial response, denying Diana the courtesies that would be extended to a true Royal and not an ex one. Holding the line most of all is Mirren, who can't quite get why the people hate her and love Diana. The underestimating of the situation leads to a national crisis, and a threat to the institution.

It isn't until Mirren drives out into her country estate late in the film and gets her car stuck that the "Cat!" moment occurs. While waiting for someone to come get her, the Queen sees a magnificent fourteen-point stag, a beautiful animal who pauses to regard her, and — when the sound of hunters approaching is heard — runs off as Mirren tells it to shoo, in the hope it will escape. At that moment, we warm to the cold Queen, and she too begins to turn in her appreciation of Diana's death.

In a movie where the main character arc is about going from someone we don't like to one we do, or at least understand, the Cat! moment comes late — but right on time for the sake of our story.

What does the deer represent? I have my own theories. But the screenwriting "trick" it exemplifies proves how even a small moment like this can turn our appreciation of a character. As screenwriters we are "emotion coordinators" — ha! I kinda like that — and the effect when done well, as it is in this case, is sublime.

The Queen is also an example of the "Institutionalized" story, in which a "Naif" (Blair) faces down the "Company Man" (The Queen et al). The showdown is reminiscent of other great conflicts of the "I" kind, including such Mentor-Mentee tales as that between Ethan Hawke and Denzel Washington in *Training Day* and even the face-off of R.P. McMurphy and Nurse Ratched in *One Flew Over The Cuckoo's Nest*.

BE BOLD
May 15, 2008

What are you afraid of?

I ask because I'm in the middle of writing *Save the Cat!* *Strikes Back* (the third and maybe best *Cat!* yet) and it suddenly occurs to me what many a movie hero has in common — at least at the start of the story — and that's fear.

Fear in a thousand forms is part of so many hero's stories when we meet them — from fear of failure revealed in a braggart (Ryan Gosling in *Fracture*) to fear of financial insecurity (when Paul Newman trolls for business at a funeral in *The Verdict*) to a funny corporate lab rat's fear of a stifling future (Ron Livingston in *Office Space*).

And each tale is the story of how the hero gets rid of that fear by confronting it.

It's one of the reasons we tell stories — so the hero can go through this horrible process for us — and we don't have to! The hero can show us how it's done.

And we get to watch and pick up tips on how he did it, all from the comfort of our plush red velvet seats.

Exploring fear in the hero of your story shows where the story really is. And making those moments ring true starts with figuring out something you might not have considered — facing your own fears!

We too are mired in fear, often hidden behind all manner of acting out. We know instinctively that our fears must be dealt with, and yet to stare down what we fear is worse than limping along with it!

Which is another reason we admire those who finally face the muzak.

The climax of many a well-told tale is that exact thing — when the hero confronts what scares him most. And as writers we can reverse engineer our stories in re-writes to make these moments even more on point. Who knows if wonderful Roy Scheider's character in *Jaws* started out "afraid of water," but it made his winding up in the drink, along with a killer shark, that much better of a story. And his deed that much greater.

And that goes for us too.

Any time we do something we think we can't, we get stronger. Facing our fears adds *gravitas* to our lives, and more to the point of this blog, to our writing. When we tap into that moment we stood up to a bully, said the glaringly obvious thing everyone else was afraid to say, or simply had faith enough to lift our foot up off the bottom of the pool and trusted we would float, we are emboldened.

And that goes right into our writing.

Take a look at a favorite movie and ask what the hero is afraid of when he starts, and how that fear is confronted. You'll be surprised. It's what explains the superhuman qualities of Bruce Willis in *Die Hard*, who isn't as afraid of dying as he is of losing his wife! It's why "fear of being ordinary" drives Peter O'Toole in *Lawrence of Arabia*, and why the outcome of that film is all the more poignant for it. It even explains silly comedies, for fear can be funny too. So long as even the silliest hero faces what he is most afraid of!

And by looking at our own fears, even minor ones, we can put that experience into our work. No, it doesn't have to be fear of bungee jumping. For you, a much more horrible fate could be public speaking, apologizing for a past misdeed, telling the truth... or showing someone your new screenplay! By looking at our fears, and facing them, we can be bold in our writing... and in life!

THE TRANSFORMATION MACHINE
August 2, 2007

All stories are about transformation.

And seeing this as a good thing is the starting point of writing a successful story of any kind.

Something has to happen, change has got to occur. That's why the opening image (the snapshot of the world BEFORE) of a movie script has to be the opposite of the final image (the snapshot of the world AFTER.)

When breaking a story that's always where I start — and what most listeners I am pitching to want to know: What HAPPENS?

Well, the way to chart that is to ask who your hero is at the start and who he is by the end.

And that's what makes Act Two what I like to call The Transformation Machine.

Heroes go into Act Two — but they don't come out. And as story-tellers, our job is to take our audience by the hand and explain that process. You the audience and I the writer, I like to say, are standing on a train platform, we're getting on the train... and we're not coming back.

The best part of the BS2, the structure strategy for breaking down these story points, is the Transformation Machine of Act Two. By charting "Fun and Games," "Midpoint," "Bad Guys Close In," "All Is Lost," and "Dark Night of the Soul," we have a map to show how that transformation occurs in our hero.

And when you add in the vital "B Story" hinge points at page 30 (when the "helper story" is introduced) to the "Midpoint" and "Break into Three" where A and B Stories cross, the meaning of this transformation is magnified.

All stories are the caterpillar turning into a butterfly in some sense. All stories require a death and rebirth to make that painful and glorious process happen.

And it occurs in movies... and in life.

We transform every day, re-awaken to new concepts about the world around us, overcome conflict, and triumph over death... only to start again each morning.

It's why stories that follow this pattern resonate. Because each day is a transformation machine, and so are our lives.

THE SHARD OF GLASS
June 22, 2009

Lately, I have been talking a lot about the "death moment" of a script. In the script consultations I do, and in class talking with groups of writers, the "All Is Lost" moment on page 75 is becoming the most important part of the story.

I'm beginning to think it's the key to cracking what your story is really about.

Since all stories are at their essence "The Caterpillar and the Butterfly," the "death moment" is the cocoon stage for your hero, where the old way dies, lies in state for a time, then breaks him out into an amazing new way of being.

It's painful, scary, and full of self-recrimination for a hero — and should be.

At the heart of that beat is the hero not only being "worse off than when this movie started" — and very often in jail, evicted, fired, abandoned, or left alone by the death of a mentor — but forced to face an ugly truth about himself that he's been resisting.

Most stories involve a blind spot or flaw the hero is not aware of. And this is the part of his transformation that is so important; it forces him to look at that flaw, usually something so buried in him that it hasn't been looked at for a long time.

That's the "shard of glass," that sharp-edged incident, bad behavior, tough truth or wrong done and absorbed that the hero swallowed a long time ago. Skin has grown up around its hard corners, but it's in there — deep — and it must be pulled out and looked at and dealt with if the hero can get to that vital butterfly stage.

In *Alien*, the "shard of glass" for Sigourney Weaver is the horrible truth that the company she believed in considers her and the crew of *Nostromo* expendable — and why they were sent on their suicide mission. In *Ordinary People*, it's when Tim Hutton rushes to his therapist to confess he's stronger than his Golden Boy brother; that's why he survived and his brother did not. In *Notting Hill*, the "shard of glass" for Hugh Grant is that it's not Julia Roberts, movie star, who's the snob, *he* is. And *he* is what has been stopping them from being together.

And it's only by having this shard pulled out of us, and examined, that we can move on to the next stage: the part where we become something glorious.

What's the "shard of glass" for your hero? What old idea must be looked at and discarded? What blind spot must your hero be forced to examine to become the fully formed being he needs to become? If you can find that shard, you can tell a more powerful story. Whether it's comedy or drama, finding that piece will make all the difference! It's not only the "cry moment" of every movie — but the truth we all get to learn from, thanks to the greatest event your hero ever experienced.

DIG DEEP DOWN
July 17, 2009

Doing a review of *Slumdog Millionaire* earlier this year, I discovered something fascinating.

We all know the movie, and the sweep of the Academy Awards® that followed its release.

But I wonder if the movie would have had the same impact if the filmmakers went with the ending the original script suggested?

In that dramatic finale, the hero played by Dev Patel "storms the castle" to get to the set of the Millionaire show and answer the final question that will make him rich. His last lifeline call goes out and by gosh SHE answers, the girl of his dreams, and the only one who can help him.

In the original script, she did! And there on the air, gave him the final answer that would solve all his problems, unite them in love... and good fortune... forever. Wow! What a happy ending!

But that's not how it went. In the movie, Dev connects to the girl of his dreams, but she doesn't know the answer. And now it's just Dev and the depth of his experience we've seen him live through where he must search for the answer. As the clock ticks, and the pressure mounts, he does.

Better?

I'd say. But why?

In my opinion, it's because that moment now delivered on a key part of what I call the "Five Point Finale," in which the hero must "Dig Deep Down" to find the answer to any problem he faces.

Dev Patel has just dug deep down as the hero of *Slumdog Millionaire*. (2008)

It's the "touched by the divine" part. And I think it made all the difference in making the ending of *Slumdog Millionaire* a success. It's that part of the story where the hero, having died at All Is Lost, now knows he is not alone. A steely pro, a hero with true — not blind — faith, he knows that if he reaches out into the darkness, someone will take his hand. Someone not necessarily human.

If you are trying to figure out that last little piece in your finale, think of the difference between being given the answer, and digging deep down to find it. This "Use the Force, Luke!" beat is why we go to the movies. When we find it, it will guide our storytelling and give it supernatural power.

ACT ONE
January 20, 2009

You will hear many writers tell you — and rightly so — that Act Three is the toughest. Finishing up what you started, finding the final solution for your characters, and also "letting them go" is a challenge for sure.

But to me, the trouble spots I see working with writers mostly are found in Act One.

Stories chart change. You begin with a hero who is one way, and by the end he is the opposite.

And yet for many reasons, we find it hard to take our heroes "all the way back" to where they need to be to show the biggest change, and the most sweeping arc.

Part of the problem, always, is we are our heroes. And if we need to show them in deficit, or even unlikeable at the beginning in order to show where they go by the end, we are wont to do so.

They're us!

And we're likeable! Why shouldn't our hero be, too?

Sometimes too, we evolve our heroes too early. We show where they will be going at the start. That is also in part because the hero is us. We don't want to see him (us) have to suffer! And we don't want to admit that he (we) needs evolving.

But that's what stories track. Change hurts. And forcing a hero to change means revealing him as embarrassingly unevolved at the start, and in need of an awakening — and the pain of changing.

If your story doesn't feel full enough, big enough, or quite on track, don't check Act Three — think about Act One. If you aren't engineering a change in the hero and his world that will be different...

Do.

ALL THE WAY BACK
July 31, 2009

Here's the problem you're confronted with: Act Three isn't gelling.

There doesn't seem to be enough *oomph* in your big finish, and the hero doesn't really seem to be learning a lesson — or applying it. That big, emotional uplift you've wanted to put in here at the end is missing. Looks like it's time to roll up your sleeves and start re-working that finale, right?

Maybe.

But maybe the real problem lies back in Act One?

In a lot of scripts I've been reading lately, finding what's wrong with the hero's story starts with how we meet him, and what his problems are up front.

And most of the time, we haven't given him enough problems to make the trip worthwhile, and the finale worthy of someone who's come so far.

The fix is to take the hero "All the Way Back" — meaning to load him up with lots of problems, both individual and systemic.

What's stopping us many times is we are our hero! And we don't like to look anything less than evolved. And like our hero, we don't want to show ourselves to seem ignorant, or problem plagued, or deficient in any way.

But we must.

This is partly about showing a complete change, and an Opening Image and Final Image that are opposites. And the pros know how to make those hero arcs big. In the Oscar*-nominated screenplay for *The Savages*, we start Laura Linney off lost in her professional life, having a tacky affair, and under the thumb of her brother, Phillip Seymour Hoffman. By the end of that movie, Laura has a play she wrote being staged, has made peace with Phillip, and traded in her lover... for his dog.

But if the screenwriter hadn't taken Laura "all the way back" to a point of desperation, and even humiliation, the finale would not be nearly as satisfying.

All we're saying is, this is about the constant adjustment of the Alpha-Omega, the change a hero undergoes. And if you're not feelin' it at the end, maybe the end isn't the problem.

HOW MUCH DO WE HAVE TO KNOW?
March 19, 2009

"Leapfrog or Box?" someone asks Clive Owen.

I am watching *Duplicity*, the new Tony Gilroy film starring Julia Roberts and Clive Owen. It's about spies. Clive is one. And he and a partner are trying to lose a "tail" following Clive on the streets of Manhattan.

"Leapfrog or Box?" he is asked again.

"Leapfrog," Clive answers.

Suddenly the move is made. Clive's partner runs interference, and Clive escapes to meet his contact.

Throughout *Duplicity*, I am dropped into the lingo and etiquette of corporate spies. And though I get the sense it's just mumbo jumbo (are there such elude-a-tail strategies?), I don't care. It's fun stuff!

And rushing to keep up with what's happening, true or not, is a big part of what makes it fun.

In my class I harp on the importance of conflict; it's what attracts our attention. And one of the best ways to increase the conflict in any movie is to make me, the audience, "lean forward" to stay with what's happening. The conflict is my need to know vs. the movie's effort to, in a sense, keep me at arm's length. And keeping me guessing beats the overkill of explaining what's happening every time.

As an audience, we do not have to know everything as it unfolds *at the exact time* it's unfolding. But what we do need to keep our eye on, and what writers must deliver, is: the bouncing ball. What's that?

When we hear a pitch, read a script, or see the finished product onscreen, the "bouncing ball" is how the hero or heroes are transforming. I am a caveman. I read 1000 different caveman details watching a movie. And in truth it's usually not the plot details, but the more primal, more human points of interest, that engage me.

I don't have to be told anything to keep up — so long as I am given a story at base about a hero who is transforming, and all the plot, all the lingo, is just on the surface of the primal part that's the real story: How does this person begin, how does he end, and why is this story we're telling "the most important event that will ever happen to him or her"?

That's all I care about. Throw jargon at me, mislead me with plot devices, dazzle me with locations, but keep me interested in the "Turn, Turn, Turn" of character change. We do not have to explain anything more.

Does *Duplicity* do that? I will leave that for you to decide. But I will say that plot-wise, detail-wise, I was just one step behind the entire time — and that's a good thing, especially in the hands of a master like Gilroy, who displayed similar technique in the brilliant *Michael Clayton*.

I wonder what "Box" is? Maybe I'll find out in *Duplicity 2*!

DID TONY SOPRANO ARC?

June 11, 2007

I don't follow the Lakers. Paris Hilton is a hotel as far as I'm concerned. I have only one rooting interest: *The Sopranos*.

Tony and Meadow and AJ and Paulie?

A religion.

So like many of you I watched the final episode last night. And I gotta say: brilliant!

Why? Because Tony does what we want all heroes of stories to do: He arcs. And though we don't get the certain "payoff" of his death, the ending creator David Chase picks instead is far more satisfying.

When we first meet Tony Soprano, he is having panic attacks. He's a mob boss in Jersey, his family is a mess, and so is his *other* family, and finding just the right therapist is tough. In the course of eight years worth of shows, Tony finds a shrink — and Prozac — puts up with his dysfunctional tribe (he being the most dysfunctional), and gets, well... better.

And unlike many who feel the last episode, in particular the last five minutes, is unresolved, I disagree. As one critic this morning said: "Tony's life will go on, we just won't get to see it." And despite the need to see him gunned down picking up the paper in his driveway by the goth son of Vito Spatafore who escapes from Outward Bound and comes back to kill the guy what sent him there (that was my bet for the ending), this finale is much more tense for having none of that.

That diner. That corny Journey song. The tension of Meadow parking her car. The series of scary hit men types coming in and out of the unfamiliar cafe where the family has gathered for onion rings, come on! Perfect! It put us in Tony's chair for one last time, weighing family ties against real life-or-death judgments.

What I love about The Sopranos, and particularly last night's episode, are the references to other movies, particularly The Godfather. The light snow flurries that sprinkle Tony and the New York crew's scenes match the chill weather when Al Pacino and Diane Keaton first see the news about Don Corleone's assassination. And last night's final scene is a reflection of Al's big moment when he takes out the police captain and the mob boss. By showing the hit men types in Tony's cafe heading to the bathroom, getting the distraction of Meadow's parallel parking problem — that parallels the roar of the El going overhead in the moments leading up to Al becoming a "made man." It all leads to a superb tension based on the clichés we've come to expect in mob fare. It is so much smarter to veer near the cliché and then step back. It shows that one of Chase's key insights is our cultural awareness of movie and TV moments, and how we expect real life to match. It is a technique he uses throughout the series, and is in evidence last night too as other TV and movie references are used for tone; I saw clips from Little Miss Sunshine and The Twilight Zone that seem to comment on the situations they are part of; the ever-present TV is always on in The Sopranos — and is always used as a brilliant counterpoint to the scene going on in the foreground.

So, what better way to say goodbye than not getting what we expected!

The fire that destroys A.J.'s car - how non-mafia can we get? And that cat! It looks like poor Paulie may never completely get rid of Christopher, as the cat implies. He may be Christ reincarnated, and vexing, spirit. Fabulous!

And the overall story is just right. The best ending is no ending. Tony changed, survived, and still has his bad eating habits (how this guy didn't get a warning from his doctor on his cholesterol level is the biggest unresolved "hit" of the series).

Bravo, David Chase. Thanks for the memories, and jeesh, don't stop believing.

Abso-friggin' lootely!

DOES WALL-E ARC?

June 11, 2007

I got an email from two writers last week asking me to settle an argument.

They had both seen the hit summer Pixar movie *WALL-E* and wondered if the hero, the lead, the namesake of the movie, does something we screenwriters try our darndest to make happen for all our heroes:

Does Wall-E arc?

The story of *WALL-E* finds its tin hero alone until he falls for a slinky fembot he goes to the ends of the universe to win. But the question is a good one, and speaks to the qualifiers of both heroes *and* arcs.

It's not about being metallic. Another animated feature, *Robots*, starring the voice of Robin Williams among others, gave its clanky characters personalities, and a full-on saga of an underdog (under robot?) sent to the big city to make good. Haley Joel Osmond in the Spielberg/Kubrick collaboration, *A.I. Artificial Intelligence*, starred as a human playing a robot, but faced similar *WALL-E*-like questions from audiences who wondered why we followed Haley to the end of time to see if he would be reunited with his "mother." If a hero is by definition not alive, can we still root for him? Artificial emotions can be as relevant as real ones — a topic explored in Philip K. Dick novel-to-films like *Blade Runner*, and to a lesser degree, *Minority Report*. But we are not as interested in the philosophical debate as we are in what this means for the rules of storytelling.

What makes us root for someone — what makes us want to see him win?

For animators trying to bring life to inanimate objects, it's all in the eyes. Emotion is found in the window to the soul; it's The Margaret Keane Effect (the kitschy artist known for little ragamuffins with big ocular orbs). In the movie *Cars*, the Pixar hit from two summers ago, the entire windshield of each character was devoted to the eyes, and each cars' grillwork was elasticized to enhance their expressions and further anthropomorphize the cast. And there was rooting interest aplenty for star voice Owen Wilson in what is essentially "*Doc Hollywood* with automobiles."

"Arc" is another matter. It's a term that basically means change. If the whole point of a story is to show transformation in a hero, if the only reason we get transformation is if something happens, then arc would seem to be a must.

We have seen human characters who by design aren't allowed to arc, do so. In *Being There*, Peter Sellers as cipher Chauncy Gardener does not cry at the start of the movie when his benefactor dies, but does shed a tear when Melvyn Douglas passes away at the end. Does Chauncy arc? Catalyst figure *Rain Man* (Dustin Hoffman) has a similar moment at the end of that film when he rests his head on Tom Cruise's shoulder, but is that a character change or an involuntary reaction? And the "save the stag!" moment Helen Mirren experiences toward the end of *The Queen* humanizes and affects the real life character depicted as "cold" until that moment in the woods, a fortuitous urging that leads to a third act change in Royal policy — and maybe a personal change in the title character.

This is not a small debate. As big a success as *WALL-E* is, it isn't generating the kind of buzz as last year's *Ratatoullie*. And as funny and wonderful an entertainment as it is, we have to wonder if we write inanimate characters, is making them capable of change — as well as root-able — a prerequisite?

Does WALL-E arc? It's a puzzle we need to solve. The mystery of how to create, enhance, and exploit rooting interest in our heroes is not only an exacting science, it's essential to the discussion about any story we write.

And one only we humans can decide!

SIMPLE TOOLS TO ENHANCE CHARACTER
January 22, 2007

I am always looking for insights into story. I listen for the mythic beats of the journey when a friend tells me about their trip to the supermarket. I watch furniture wax commercials on TV and look for the "arc" of the housewife/protagonist (believe me, it's in there). The point is: There are lessons in the simplest stories. And they are often easiest to see in comedies — which is why I tend to reference them.

While watching the movie version of *The Producers: The Musical*, I noticed one such lesson. This is the movie based on the musical based on the movie. (Is there another example of this ever happening?) I never saw the Broadway version (although I did catch the road company production featuring Erik Estrada and "Screech" from *Saved by the Bell*), but from the first movie starring Zero Mostel and Gene Wilder to this one starring Nathan Lane and Matthew Broderick, there were a few notable changes in the story.

Let's start with the fact that both versions are funny. One is a raw, flat-out comedy spoof with an almost "Indie" feel, while the musical is bigger, more fleshed out, and more "whole." You will never be able to repeat the experience of seeing "Springtime for Hitler" for the first time, but it's interesting to see how the musical enhanced what were very simple characters in the original — and boosted the story as a result.

For one, they gave accountant Leo Bloom much more of a role in the musical. When Matthew walks into the offices of the washed-up Bialystock Productions, he has something Gene didn't: In his wallet is a ticket to a performance he saw as a kid of one of Nathan's earlier hit shows! Not only is Matthew a fan, he offers Nathan a callback to his more successful days. Matthew also has a second thing Gene Wilder didn't have in the original: a specific dream. Matthew has always had a secret desire to be a Broadway producer (thus the ticket in his wallet), so when he is offered the chance by Nathan, it's more than just a scheme to make money. And it also leads to one of the most fun musical numbers, "I Want to be a Producer," set in Matthew's accounting offices. Finally, in the musical version, Matthew also has one other thing: a woman problem; he is painfully, terminally shy. In the musical, that is solved too when Ula (in the original just a sight gag) arrives and has a more important role (played in this version by Uma Thurman) and is the love story with Nathan as observer.

The result: *The Producers: The Musical* has really become much more Matthew's story, an interesting shift from the original film.

Why bring this up? When fleshing out heroes of stories, my question to any writer is: What does your hero want? I always ask the writer to be specific, because what a hero wants is the hero's character — and it is also the story! And while the musical version of the cult classic may not be a better version of *The Producers* (nothing can compete with Zero Mostel, who was more a force of nature), in fleshing out a story and making it whole, it is a more complete version. Think about what writers Mel Brooks and Thomas Meehan did that the divine Brooks, the sole original writer, left out of the original film.

The changes are more satisfying in terms of understanding the theme of the story and a great lesson in rewriting: When you are told your characters are a little "two-dimensional," think about wants, needs, goals — and "Bialystock & Bloom."

SPINOFF: THE CONTEST
August 14, 2008

One of the exciting things about being a movie fan is the potential to dig deeper into the imaginary lives of the characters we meet onscreen — even if that meeting is brief.

There is a chance that we will see a movie 10 or 20 times during our lives. And I'm convinced that the success of "chopping up time" in movies like *Pulp Fiction* is due to our now commonplace habit — mine anyway — to see a movie on cable in chunks. Very often I will see a new movie by catching a bit of the middle, filling in the end later, and finally seeing the beginning some other time... and still get it.

One of my favorite pastimes, as I watch a movie more than once, is thinking about its minor characters. Whatever happened to Serge from *Beverly Hills Cop*? The espresso-wielding omni-sexual Serge launched the career of Bronson Pinchot, and is one of the great character turns ever. But while we know Bronson starred in a fun TV series, Serge disappeared, even though he made a brief appearance in a later *Cop* installment.

Whatever happened to him?

We see this on TV too. Or don't see it. The elusive Marris, Niles' (David Hyde Pierce) wife on *Frasier* never was seen, although the theater of the mind filled in all kinds of pictures of her. The neighbor on *Tim Allen's Home Improvement* went to great lengths to stay off camera, too.

But as I go deeper into more and more viewings of certain films, 10 or 20 times down the road, all kinds of questions come to mind: Whatever happened to Bruno Kirby and Carrie Fisher in *When Harry Met Sally...* Did they go the distance as a married couple? And what about the great lover Wallace Shawn portrayed in *Manhattan*, the one that so surprised Woody Allen when he and Diane Keaton ran into him while shopping? Did he and Diane ever get together again for one tumultuous sexual romp?

If you've ever wondered about the lives of these minor characters prior to the entry into our lives, or what happened to them after the movie was over, here's your chance to let your imagination run wild.

1. Take a well-known movie and pick a minor character — or one that is referenced yet never seen.

2. Make him or her the star of a new movie in which we answer the question: What happened to them AFTER the movie? or Where did he or she come from, and what were they doing BEFORE the movie began?

3. Pick a title that vaguely smacks of that of the original movie and...

4. Write a logline of that movie.

EXAMPLE:

KEYSER PERMANENTE — Sequel to *The Usual Suspects* finds its disgraced police captain (Chazz Palminteri) busted down to an HMO hospital security detail, until a series of murders in the Physical Therapy unit — and another broken coffee cup — draw him back into a case that still might be solved.

Whether you know it or not, these fun little contests are the "Wax on, Wax off" exercises that help us stretch some very important muscles. Not only do we practice writing better loglines, but by addressing the confines of an "assignment" that is so like others we will face in our careers, the skills to "Give me the same thing, only different!" are strengthened. And having just seen the play *Wicked* for the first time recently —the "prequel" of how the Wicked Witch of the West came to be in *The Wizard of Oz* — it's not out of the range of possibility that this exercise could lead to similar success. It's a great thought-starter for sure!

CHAPTER 6

June 4, 2007
"As to structure? It is THE KEY to telling a good story."

STRUCTURE

WHY CLEAR STORY STRUCTURE = CLEAR THINKING
April 16, 2009

One thing I hear from audiences I get to speak to, from writers in class or in email from readers who are having a light-bulb moment from reading my books, is how learning story structure has changed their lives.

And I couldn't be happier — or more grateful — than to share in these eyes-wide-open hazzahs!

When you work out the "beats" of a story via the Beat Sheet (a free download available in the Tools section of www.savethecat.com) or in our software, structure leads to clear thinking.

Being able to "see" a story as we write it is why we use these templates. All stories are about "transformation," so our job is to tell the tale that has the biggest possible change. When we look at the Opening Image that starts a story and hold it up against the Final Image, we must make sure those two points are... opposite. And the "Transformation Machine" that all good stories measure tracks this change.

I say it all the time in class: It's easy.

And powerful.

If we can tell a story well, we can communicate on every level in a quicker, more effective way!

Yet the structure method we use is more than that: it's fresh air for the mind. So often our imaginations get cluttered. Some of the pictures in our head are totally 100% right-on. But some are just clutter. And having a story clothesline to hang our thoughts on, look at them, and have others be able to look too, empowers every storyteller with a method to not only communicate what's in our minds, but test to see if what we're communicating makes sense to someone who isn't inside our heads — and that's invaluable!

Story is puzzle solving. And having not only the perspective but the cool aplomb to know our idea doesn't have to be perfect the first time leads to even greater exercise of our gray matter.

Whether you wind up as a professional storyteller, or as someone creating a 30-second TV commercial, or giving a speech to the PTA, or any of a thousand ways "story" is used to communicate, you are better empowered to tell your story if you think of the "Transformation Machine" our story templates help you create. From uninformed to informed, from apathetic to involved, from feeling superior to feeling humbled (and thus ready to be called to a higher purpose), transformation is our business.

And there is no better way to look at every article we write, speech we give, or message we articulate, than by the clear thinking it takes to deliver on the 15 beats — these little turnstiles of change — of every story we tell!

MORE PATTERNS, MORE A-HA! MOMENTS
December 3, 2007

The great part about teaching is the teacher keeps learning.

And you never know when the lesson will strike.

If I suddenly look like I'm listening to a far-off dog whistle, head cocked, slightly blank expression, repeating something I said a moment ago, odds are you are witnessing that very moment.

But such is the unpredictability of the "A-ha!" experience.

One insight hit me recently while talking about the "Fun and Games" section of a movie (the aptly titled part that occurs right at the start of Act Two) when I suddenly realized this amazing bit:

Fun and Games = Your Pitch!

The "Fun and Games" section contains the "promise of the premise" and that means it's also the poster of your movie. So when Tom Cruise, as future cop John Anderton in *Minority Report*, FINALLY jumps into action when he discovers the suspect in a future crime is him... well, guess what? That's the logline.

And if you're trying to figure out what your movie is, or when the crux of the plot starts, this factoid is a really important thing to know.

Another "A-ha!" occurred during a break from our Master Class this weekend (an amazing group btw). I, and two graduates of the Cat! class, were discussing *Shaun of the Dead* when we were reminded of a key factor that makes that sci-fi comedy a winner. I call it the "Emotional Color Wheel" in *Save the Cat!* and it really applies to this movie. *Shaun of the Dead* works because the writers have made a point not to be funny in every scene. Sure it's a funny situation, but it's also scary as hell in places as when the brain-eating zombies attack Sean and friends in their pub. It even gets downright emotional when Sean must deal with his less-than-proud mother. But because the movie isn't one-note emotionally, it feels like these weird events are real. And thus Sean's transformation from zero to hero is real, too.

Perhaps the best A-ha! happened while teaching here in L.A. recently when, standing at the white board with my structure map, I had a true breakthrough about the overall function of story. Look at how the Catalyst – Debate – Break into Two sequence in Act One is identical to All Is Lost – Dark Night of the Soul – Break into Three that occurs toward the end of Act Two. Both Catalyst and All Is Lost are something done to the hero; the hero's response in both cases is the "debate" about what he must do next; and the Break into Two or Three is what that action entails!

And in each case an old way of life, or an old idea, dies!

The difference is: in the latter set of plot points, the stakes are bigger, it's "life and death" and must be because, as I keep being reminded, all stories are about transformation – and a big part of that is sloughing off the old to make way for the new.

This cycle is one we see in life, too, and that may be the ultimate A-ha! Think about the 15 beats as they apply to a day of your life sometime and see how from the Opening Image (opening your eyes when you wake up) to the Final Image (closing your eyes when you go to sleep) the 15 beats match many of the ups and downs of your waking hours, and how some kind of "transformation" occurs by day's end. It's why stories that follow this pattern hit home. They resonate because we recognize them from our own life experience.

Finding these patterns gives us the keys to success as writers. We aren't about "formula," we are about essence! And the search for the subterranean meaning of why stories work never ends.

Like my job? Nope. I LOVE it! I hope I always keep finding new things.

THE STORY SPINE
April 21, 2008

In the first *Save the Cat!*[*] I propose that every good tale hits the 15 beats of my beat sheet, the infamous BS2! But I now propose further that Step One of any story breaking adventure must begin with only three of those points: The Opening Image, The Final Image, and The Midpoint.

These three points block out what your story will be.

How does this movie begin and how does it end? That's the key to finding the Opening Image and the Final Image. It's what I call "snipping the ends" of the story... and it couldn't be more vital. After coming up with the idea and logline for your script, answering this question is the next step.

In the beginning of *Liar Liar*, Jim Carrey is a liar; by the end he's not. What happened? In the Opening Image of *Sleepless in Seattle* Tom Hanks and his son are burying his dead wife; in the Final Image, Tom and his son walk off with Meg Ryan. Wow! Something big went on there, a complete reversal! This drastic change, these opposites, MUST be huge, upside-down, night and day differences. It's a difference that we need as an audience — otherwise why invest in the hero's journey?

As to the Midpoint, this continues to be the nerve center of any script for me, with more and more "things" adding to its mystique. If you can crack the Midpoint, you've cracked the story. Just look at all the things that happen there: It's where there's either a "false victory" or a "false defeat"; it's where the "stakes are raised" and "time clocks" appear; it's where the Bad Guys learn the Good Guy's secret (*Die Hard*) or his whereabouts (*Witness, E.T.*); it's where the boy and girl kiss for the first time (Sex at 60!); where big parties and events announce the hero getting "everything he thought he wanted" (*Bruce Almighty*) or in the event of a "false defeat," take that same totality away (*Legally Blonde* — remember Elle Woods in her bunny ears?)

And it is EVER thus: be it indie, big-budget blockbuster or sitcom — crack the Midpoint, crack the story.

Those three points constitute the "spine" and must be addressed first. After coming up with the killer idea, breaking out these three points guarantees success.

I bring this easy method to writers who want to win in this, the greatest time ever to be a writer with a vision! With more opportunity than has ever been available before, how can we fail?!

So long as we keep on our mission — good stories, well told — we too will win every time.

FINDING THE SPINE
October 20, 2008

When it comes to fixing broken scripts, your story's "spine" is key. Avoiding story "scoliosis" — a crooked tale of missteps and detours — is the name of the game.

The spine of your story is defined as what happens to your hero as we chart his transformation from the start of your tale to its finish. The demarcations of growth that hero goes through IS the story. And tracking how he changes is your main job.

A quick 5-question checklist to make sure your story spine is straight includes:

1. Who's your hero? Not always easy to answer — especially if you're penning a "buddy movie" or an ensemble piece, but until you know, how will you be able to "follow the bouncing ball" that is the point of the tale?

2. How does this story begin and how does it end? To show growth you must "snip the ends" properly to show an Opening Image and a Final Image that are opposites. But is this the biggest change it can be?

3. What's the problem? Not only does your hero have to have a whole bunch of personal "things that need fixing" but so does the world he lives in. And how will those problems eventually get fixed?

4. What is the tangible goal and what is the spiritual goal of your

story? This is the A Story and the B Story, better known as the "wants" and "needs" of your hero, and finally...

5. What's it about? This is the theme... and without knowing what that is, you will get lost along the way.

These five simple questions aren't always easy to answer, but all address the key question: What's your story spine? If you have answers, you are more likely to tell a better story — and not stray into the weeds.

SYNTHESIS
September 9, 2006

The rule of threes is a part of many artistic endeavors.

In a joke, the punchline always comes with the third example.

In popular music, like a Beatles tune, it's the hook sung by Paul, the "middle eight" bars of the chorus sung by John, and a return to the hook, usually with Paul and John singing together.

And in screenwriting it's Act One, Act Two, and Act Three. But what happens in Three must have what the joke or the pop tune has: synthesis.

You may call it Act One – Act Two – Act Three. I call it Thesis – Anti-thesis – Synthesis.

And this Hegelian triumvirate is crucial to satisfying storytelling.

In Act One of *Titanic* for instance, the Thesis world is Rose (Kate Winslet) about to marry the wrong man.

In Act Two, the Anti-thesis, Rose falls for Jack Dawson (Leonardo diCaprio) and the "upside-down version of the world" includes them exploring all levels of the ship and their future... up until both strike an iceberg.

In Act Three, with the ship sunk, and Leo dead, the lone survivor, Rose, is asked by officials for her name. "Rose Dawson" is her answer.

Blake breaks the three acts into 15 beats.

The perfect Synthesis beat!

Rose took what she was in Act One, combined it with what she learned in Act Two, to create a third way, a synthesis of the two!

And examples of these "Synthesis" moments are found in lots of Act Threes.

In *10*, starring Dudley Moore, Act One is Dud in midlife crisis, with a girlfriend, Julie Andrews, he can't commit to.

In Act Two, Dud chases Bo Derek, and learns from her the love-making magic of Ravel's "Bolero."

And in Act Three, Dudley comes home, his midlife crisis over, and guess what the last beat is? Dudley making love to Julie to the sounds of "Bolero." He took what he started with in 1, combined it with what he learned in 2, and found a third way, a new way.

Dudley's transformation is complete, and so is his story.

You must find the Synthesis beat in your own stories too. Without it, it's a less satisfying journey.

The Synthesis beat shows that we can all learn from our mistakes, no matter how embarrassing, and triumph in the end because of them.

WE GET LETTERS...
March 26, 2007

Let me just say up front: I love you guys! The very best by-product of writing *Save the Cat!* is the fact I get to meet so many great writers all over the world who read my book and contact me via email.

Here is one letter from a writer who has read *Cat!* and written a script using the BS2:

Hi Mr. Snyder,

I keep looking back at my older scripts, and my first and second scripts are ... well at least they're formatted correctly. But on my third, the one I first emailed you about set-up/set pieces, something just didn't seem right. So, I went through and read it 3 times, and I realized that the way I had it was that the DNOTS (Dark Night of the Soul) comes before the All is lost scene. I won't say it seems horribly out of place or forced, but I don't think that it gives the DNOTS scene enough "umph."

So, do you think this warrants a restructuring/rewriting of those two scenes, or can this happen and be passably acceptable?

Here's my reply:

Thanks for writing me and congrats on working the methods of STC! This topic is one that comes up a lot in the workshops I teach. Here's what I like to say about the All Is Lost/Dark Night of the Soul/ Break into Three in class.

All stories are about transformation. Let's start there. This is why the BS2 is so important — and so natural. The BS2 is just a way to "check your math" to make sure you are showing this transformation. You start off every story with the Opening Image: the hero as he is BEFORE this movie starts, and end with the Final Image: the hero AFTER. And the two should show a drastic change, e.g, a loser becomes a hero, a liar becomes a truth teller, etc.

What happens in between to make this change possible? Part of any transformation is the death of something, and it occurs in my beat sheet on roughly page 75 of most scripts in what I call the All Is Lost beat. But the process of something dying and being reborn is what this part of the transformation is really all about.

Think about a caterpillar that transforms into a butterfly. At some point there is a stirring in that nonwinged creature, a sense of discomfort, a "disturbance in the force," and part of that process is pain. Letting go of what was, and what one feels safe being, is scary as hell! And part of the surrender of realizing you have no control over this change is a "death" in itself. That death has to happen first. It's The End of the way it was.

What follows immediately after is natural and just as commonsensical: Now what? What was is dead. But what's ahead is unclear. That moment too has to be charted and shown in a kind of cocoon stage. The netherworld of being neither caterpillar nor butterfly is the Dark Night of the Soul moment. What will happen next? We don't know. And this moment MUST follow All Is Lost; to precede it makes no sense.

And then... hazzah!... a new stirring. The Break into Act Three is that moment, inside the cocoon when the hero decides to be a third thing: butterfly. Literally being reborn after this horrible, uncertain dark night is what makes the "Synthesis" in Act Three possible — the exploration of this third way that is a combination of the world as it was in Act One, and the world that is the upside-down version of it that's seen in Act Two, now becomes something brand new in Act Three. 1 + 2 = 3 is the math of this formula.

It is found in nature and in art. And in a good, well-structured screenplay.

It is a rhythm we understand because we too have been reborn many times in our lives. More importantly, it FEELS right, doesn't it? And that's why these three beats come in quick succession — and in order.

Hope that helps.

Sincerely,
Blake Snyder

THE THREE WORLDS OF "WANTED"

June 30, 2008

You may call it Act 1, Act 2, and Act 3, but I call 'em "Thesis," "Anti-thesis," and "Synthesis."

The three worlds of a screenplay are just that — different places with different demands. When deconstructing a script in class, or in a studio consultation, this is where I always start: the big picture, the overview. Examining the "three worlds" not only shows "How does it begin and how does it end?", it reveals the process of the hero's "transformation" in a way that is the starting point of any discussion about "fixing" a script. A good example of the "three worlds" in action is seen in the #2 movie of the weekend, *Wanted*.

Wanted is fun action picture, and while I shy away from movies that encourage their teen audience to shoot people as a way to get results (*Grand Theft Auto IV* dude, about as scary as it gets), there is a style to the violence that is new and terribly intoxicating. But as a structuralist, I am most concerned with how it works.

Wanted works like *Matrix*. A naif, an innocent, a cubicle dweller with a dead-end life, is told on page 12 that in fact he is a natural born assassin. After the normal guy's hesitancy to join up — even though doing so means hanging out with Angelina Jolie — our hero succumbs and his training begins. This section is just part of the "upside-down version of the world," the Anti-thesis of everything our hero, and we, think of as "normal." And "training" is always a big part of any "Fun and Games" rise to the "false victory" of Midpoint.

And yet, the funhouse-mirror reflection characters that appear here are just like those Dorothy finds in *The Wizard of Oz*. What were farmhands and mean teachers and sideshow medicine men become in the "Anti-thesis" world scarecrows and wicked witches and wizards. So it is in *Wanted*, as our hero finds a whole new pecking order at "work." If he thought being a cubicle dweller was tough, his coffee breaks now include dips in a pool of electrolytes to speed recovery from his knife cuts and broken bones.

But that's World Two for ya. And "Anti-thesis" is just the beginning of change this hero will undergo. It's like *Training Day*, in that regard, in which we begin the movie with an "ethical" but naive hero, throw him into the upside-down world where the rules no longer apply, and now force him to choose a "third way."

And again, just like *Training Day*, when that world proves to be false, and falsely embracing, we must change yet again. In *Wanted*'s "All Is Lost" the hero (James McAvoy) is "worse off than when this movie started" and the "whiff of death" includes almost being killed while losing the "mentor" that didn't seem to be so when we first met him. The compare-and-contrast between these two dead teachers in *Training Day* (Scott Glenn) and *Wanted* (Thomas Kretschmann) tells us how very similar these two stories are too.

The "third way" the hero seeks is a combination of what he was and what he's learned. The hero can no longer go back to the life he had before, but he can't stay where he is either. In the "netherworld" of "Dark Night of the Soul," he must find a new answer — and he does! *Wanted*'s Act Three "Synthesis" includes the "Five Point Finale" and a "Storming the Castle" sequence that actually is a castle! Love it when that happens!

By the end, *Wanted*'s hero is "transformed" having crossed through three worlds: Thesis - Anti-thesis - Synthesis. Yes, the special effects are great, yes, the story is compelling, but it's this transformation that makes it the most satisfying part of any movie, and what we all — audience and writer — seek.

BATMAN BY THE BEATS
July 24, 2008

The *Dark Knight* is the most successful movie of the year, besting *Spider-Man 3* for the biggest non-holiday opening ever. Heath Ledger is so very weird as the Joker, and the movie's highlight. But the star is a well-structured story. This latest Batman follows the beats down to the minute and delivers a resonating theme missing from other summer fare: Why is good good? And why should we try to save a world that no longer cares?

Spoiler alert: let's take a look.

The Set-up finds Gotham plagued by a new crime wave, and Batman (Christian Bale), still dark after all these years, bugged by Comic-con copycats and getting no respect as usual. The Stasis = Death is clear early on: Mansion-less, friend-less, tired of the grind — if things don't change, Bruce Wayne will "die."

The Catalyst comes when the Joker's criminal actions are brought to the attention of Batman and the world, and after some Debate about how he will enter the fray, Batman "takes the case" at the Break into Act Two.

The Fun and Games follow with Joker running amok among the crime world, rising to fame as Batman tries to catch up. Each of Joker's appearances top the last; he is pure evil. The stakes raise at a Midpoint party (amazing) when the Joker appears in Bruce Wayne's world and the two meet for the first time. The Midpoint cross of A and B, however, involves Bruce, and Rachel (Maggie Gyllenhaal) and Harvey Dent (Aaron Eckhart).

Harvey (and by extension Rachel) is the B Story, the "helper story" that will help Batman "get" what this latest crime spree is really all about. Harvey is the soul that Batman and Joker battle over, and tear right down the middle, literally, when he becomes "Two Face" in a really lovely — and gruesome — twist.

This "worse off than when this movie started" moment occurs right on schedule at All Is Lost with the death of Rachel and the maiming of Harvey, followed by a classic Dark Night of the Knight when the world's most famous butler (Michael Caine) finds Bruce slumped in his chair wondering, what's it all about, Alfie?

But because superheroes are compelled to do right, even at the risk to, and sacrifice of, themselves (check out Chapter 10 of *Save the Cat!* *Goes to the Movies*), Batman must stop Joker in the Finale that is textbook "Storming the Castle." Its "Dig Deep Down" beat comes as a result of a "divine intervention" when, given the chance to blow up a boatload of prisoners to save themselves, Gotham citizens choose not to. Yes, there is a Good. And there is a reason to fight the Evil that is Joker — even if it means more self-sacrifice — and even if Joker never dies. That after all is the point, and the eternal problem: Batman will always be on call.

So, riding off into the Dark Knight, hounded by hounds, Batman will just have to keep doing what he does. But he's been oddly re-booted for the task, and given proof, thanks to Harvey and the citizens of Gotham, that there's a reason good is good. And no copycat can take on the task that Batman now must face alone.

It's not the car chases, it's not Heath, it's not the cool new motor-cycle... it's the story. Plot and theme are blended together as the A and B Stories, and for a so-called comic book movie, it's "about something."

Now regarding Batman's voice....

THE BOARD SAYS YES... OR NOT QUITE YET
February 13, 2007

We had another amazing workshop this past weekend. This was the Master Class where writers who have gone through the torture of one of my previous boot camps bring in the 15 beats of their movie and attempt to turn them into the 40 scenes necessary to start writing the script itself.

But when we put the 40 cards of our screenplay outline up on The Board and pitch it to the rest of the workshop, that's where the vulcanized plant material meets the macadam. Suddenly the chinks in our mental image of a perfect and perfectly comprehensible movie reveal themselves. Where is the story? Who are these people you want us to follow? And why should we care? What's missing becomes obvious... fast.

So often it gets down to a clear Set-up. The first row of cards laid out by writers showing that chunk of screenplay between the Opening Image and the Break into Act Two is usually the thing that needs the most clarity. Setting up the story with a hero we like, and demonstrating what he wants, the Six Things That Need Fixing he must overcome, and figuring out the difference between the Catalyst (something happening TO the hero on page 12) and the Act Break (something the hero actively DOES to take us into a new world) is crucial to see.

And almost always it starts out muddy.

We need a clear cut scene to meet the hero. Who is he? And what is his world? We need a clear Theme Stated scene where you declare what your movie is about. And we need to root for him. Thus *Save the Cat!* What is that scene or character quality that makes me in the audience say, I like this guy... or at least understand him!

Everyone in the class got better. Some got up to The Board four or five times during the weekend, and what a learning curve! I particularly loved seeing a writer go from taking a paragraph to describe what happens in each scene to a couple of sentences... because they'd finally figured out what HAD to happen. By Sunday night, it was boom-boom-boom as writers clearly and concisely pitched their scripts. Suddenly they knew what it was... where maybe they hadn't before.

I would love to get into a workshop with everyone in the *STC!* universe. It's such a great feat of mental acuity. But barring that, there are things you can do to have this experience.

Here's my suggestion: If you have a writing group that meets regularly, take turns pitching your movies by demonstrating all 40 of your scenes on The Board. It's not only a great test of where your story is, but gets you out of your head and forces you to stand by (literally) the pictures of your imagination you thought were perfect!

This is the exact same tool used forever in the studio offices of writers, directors, editors, and executives. And it's a puzzle-solving skill we can get better at with practice. You break 10 stories and you will start to get what this is about. Break 100 and you'll see how far you have to go. Break 1000 and suddenly the light starts to go on. This is do-able! And this is fun! You get better every time out. But you have to do it. The Board is the best tool you can use to tell if you are ready to launch into FADE IN... or not quite there yet!

BLOCKBUSTER

June 13, 2006

When a movie is a hit, we call it a blockbuster. But when a screenwriter is experiencing a block, or has reached the Dark Night of the Script (as we all must before the triumphant Break into Three!), we need to bust that block. Well, I have found the way!

This week in class we had one writer who needed help with his script. The Fun and Games section of his story, a heist tale, was not working. And his Bad Guys seemed pale.

So... we broke up into groups.

And started making lists.

One group made a list of possible ways the heist could take place, who and what was guarding the "castle" that was about to be robbed, what new types of guard dogs could be put on post to protect it.

The other group thought of characters: Who was the Bad Guy? What did he want? Who was on his team of underlings? Should we name the love interest Colette or Olivia? And how could we give each character a unique "limp and eye patch" to make them pop off the screen.

When separated from the plot, or the need to keep the plot in mind, the list-making exercise was just fun. We could pitch anything, try everything. We even stopped the activity for a moment and said: "Okay, now let's come up with all the bad ideas we can think of, what should never go into a movie like this?"

And we made a list of those, too.

Result: the world's fastest fix of a story. The switch of left brain to right brain (I think I got that correct), the abandoning of the need to address the linear plot and just be creative, broke through the block — and some of the ideas we came up with that should never go into a movie like this... wound up being the freshest of the session.

While you may not have a group of eager writers at your beck and call, you can still stop and make lists. You can abandon the need to be smart, and just be creative in problem solving.

Your blockbuster may be just that if you try to bust your block the right way... and the wrong way too! It works.

I picked Colette by the way. A great name for a love interest!

DOUBLE MUMBO JUMBO MUDDLE

January 24, 2006

I propose that as an audience we can only buy one piece of magic per movie. You cannot have aliens land and then be bitten by vampires and become both alien and undead. Not fair. That to me is a "cheat" in writing and disses viewers. I call it Double Mumbo Jumbo.

My best example of DMJ is *Dreamcatcher*, the movie based on the Stephen King book (so even my heroes can go over the line) which is an example of Quadruple Mumbo Jumbo in my opinion. This is due to its use of e.s.p., aliens, germ warfare, AND predicting the future. To me, it's too much to "buy." The resulting film is very confusing.

And yet...

I have gotten into some very interesting discussions lately about the piling on of "magic" in a movie. What will we buy? And what does it take to sell more than one piece of magic? Are *Star Wars* and *Star Trek* examples of "cheating" due to their use of both sci-fi futuristics AND mysticism? And what about *Spider-Man*? Does its twin creation myths where we see both Spidey and Green Goblin "born" by two different sets of magic bug you as much as it bugs me?

I am dead smack in the middle of writing the chapter in my new book about Out of the Bottle movies, those films that use "magic," so it's very pertinent. I am covering *Freaky Friday*, *Cocoon*, *Nutty Professor*, *What Women Want*, and *Eternal Sunshine of the Spotless Mind*. All examples of various kinds of magic. So far, I've found one example of DMJ among these — the scene in *What Women Want* when Mel Gibson first gets his powers to hear what women are thinking. As he walks through the park, a dog passes, a female dog, a female French poodle in fact, whom Mel overhears speaking — in a French accent.

It is definitely an example of piling one talent (hearing women's thoughts) on top of another (hearing what dogs are thinking) — and with an accent!

Is this fair game? Is this just a cute throwaway gag? Do we care?

So you can see the kinds of things that keep ME up at night!

SPEEDED UP: FASTER MOVIES, BETTER STORIES?
May 12, 2008

This was movie weekend for me! And wasn't I glad to be back at the Octoplex!

Early on, that's how I spent most weekends: seeing lots of movies. I'd go downtown early on Saturday, stay all day, check out three, four, five films (plus the trailers), and even "interview" other moviegoers during the breaks just to see if they saw what I saw.

I recommend this still. Not many careers offer the ability to meet the target market so easily.

If there's one thing we can do to get better at this it's: Know thy audience!

This weekend I saw only two movies (lazybones that I am): *Ironman* and *Forgetting Sarah Marshall*. Liked 'em both! And throughout both, as is my habit nowadays, all I kept thinking was: *there's-the-fun-and-games-there's-the-midpoint-there's-the-all-is-lost-a-ha!* Third-Act-Synthesis — nice!

It's an occupational hazard. But a fun one!

And very edifying!

The 15 beats of the BS2 can easily be found in both these films. And *Ironman* (the #1 film two weekends in a row) clearly hits every beat (spoiler alert!). I particularly loved the Midpoint of *Ironman* which covered pretty much everything identified in *Save the Cat!*® including: a Midpoint party scene, "false victory" of Robert Downey Jr. (great in this!) successfully flying around LA in the scene just before, near kiss with Gwyneth Paltrow (A and B Story cross), plus a "raise the stakes" reveal of Jeff Bridges as the "bad guy" with Bad

Guys Close In, and the All Is Lost "whiff of death" (Downey actually dies and comes back in this particular page 75) close at hand.

These very same beats can be found in *Sarah Marshall*.

They can be found in all successful stories be they Indie, big tentpole movie, or featurette.

The big difference I saw this weekend however was... more scenes! The pace in each of these films is faster than I've ever noticed, with more half-scenes, mini-scenes, flashbacks, cut to's, cutaways, and point-of-view shifts than any movie I can point to of late.

If you don't think the pacing of movies has changed, and can evolve still more, take a look at the languid rollout of most movies pre-1990. Audiences steeped in cinema, and ahead of us screenwriters, get it! Faster, slicker, and quicker than before.

And as the writers of said films, we must adapt.

And yet!

The most human, poignant moments from both these films are what each story is really about — and the moments that make each work. *Sarah Marshall* was especially successful, and in every way broke our pre-conceived notions of stereotype. I really recommend this film as an example of "the same thing only different"; it's so like the movie *10*, starring Dudley Moore, and yet brand new.

The structure for these "speeded-up movies" remains the same, and the requirements of each section of the beat sheet is, too.

THE FIVE-STEP FINALE
December 17, 2007

My 15-point beat sheet is proving to be the secret weapon of story-tellers everywhere.

One person explained the success of this and other *Cat!* tools by relating a key moment in the evolution of the sport of scuba diving.

Huh?

That's what *I* said when he told me.

But what my friend went on to explain makes total sense.

Up until the 1960s, he said, scuba diving was considered too intimidating for the average person. You had to be a Navy seal, or a millionaire, to participate. Then two guys developed what became known as the PADI method (google for further info) that changed all that. Thereafter both grandmas and little kids could take a 30-minute lesson at Club Med and soon be in the swim. The method makes scuba diving open to everyone via its simplicity, and mostly — it takes the fear out of it!

That's what *Cat!* has done. Screenwriting doesn't have to be the Temple of Doom. You don't have to be a Jedi Master to enjoy it. And *Cat!* does not boom at you with the stentorian warning of: You'll never be good at this, consider yourself lucky to even be here!

We say: Welcome! Bien venu! Come on in!

The water's fine!

In my now much-touted beat sheet, point #14, however, may seem a little too simple. I call it "Finale" and in the book I suggest you use it to finalize the arc of your hero and "sum up all your B, C, and D stories." (Well, thanks a pantload, Blake!)

But in teaching *Cat!* classes these last two years I realize I've had a little trick all along that I should have disclosed in the book.

I call it "The Five-Step Finale." And I use it all the time.

For those of you wondering how to end your story, and what needs to get done in Act Three, try this:

Think of every Finale in terms of "storming the castle."

Step 1: The hero, and the hero's team, come up with a plan to "storm the castle" and "free the princess" who is "trapped in the tower."

Step 2: The plan begins. The wall of the castle is broached. The heroes enter the Bad Guy's fort. All is going according to plan.

Step 3: Finally reaching the tower where the princess is being kept, the hero finds... she's not there! And not only that, it's a trap! It looks like the Bad Guy has won.

Step 4: The hero now has to come up with a new plan. And it's all part and parcel of the overall transformation of the hero and his need to "dig deep down" to find that last ounce of strength (i.e., faith in an unseen power) to win the day.

Step 5: Thinking on the fly, and discovering his best self, the hero executes the new plan, and wins! Princess freed, friends avenged, Bad Guy sent back to wherever Bad Guys go when they are defeated (Two Bunch Palms?) — our hero has triumphed.

This 5-step sequence can be seen in *Gladiator*, *Die Hard*, *Star Wars*, and recently in *Enchanted*. But in truth it is the basis of many finales. It doesn't have to be an action hero or involve a castle to work. But it's a quick way to find what your story is really about! As I say in the blog I wrote for the Writers Store called "The Moment of Clarity," all stories are about being touched by the transforming power of the divine, and the Five-Step Finale is a quick and easy way to synthesize that.

Try it and see! And happy scuba diving! I mean... screenwriting!

p.s. Saw *I Am Legend* Friday at The Grove in Los Angeles! And there is a moment right up front when star Will Smith actually saves a cat! (Even though the cat is the lion cub of a predator who wants the deer good Will is hunting, it's in there for only one reason: to show why we should like the hero!)

Blake's iMac, ready for its close-up.

IN MY QUEUE 2

August 30, 2007

It's the last hot and hazy week of summer. Big things are about to happen this coming crisp and cool fall. And I can't wait!

So what movies am I watching in my spare time?

Here is the list of films I've been screening that will tell you where my brain is these days.

The first category of film I've been enjoying is subtitled. Yup. I have been watching and in some cases re-watching some classic French films lately, enjoying the onscreen smoking of Gauloise and the free-wheelin' use of the word "merda" even in 1948.

Bob Le Flambeur

Pepe le Moko

Shoot the Piano Player

Touchez Pas au Grisbi

What is the explanation for this foreign film jag? Is it the recent warming of Franco-American relations, the skyrocketing sales of *Save the Cat!** in France? The love of rich sauces? Well, partly.

I look at these French gangster pictures for inspiration. So essentially we're going back to the well to see if there isn't some other black-and-white foreign film that can inspire us again.

All of the above are just that. From the Truffaut classic, *Shoot the Piano Player*, to the moody-cool *Bob*, we're seeing why structure, or the lack thereof, is important.

And all are ripe for re-interpretation.

Also in my cue is a whole raft of documentaries. I have been toying with the idea of writing a book that applies the BS2 to non-fiction — and trust me it does. From the "Save the Cat" moment to the "All Is Lost" beat (including the "whiff of death"), successful documentaries also follow the BS2. If you don't believe me, here is my queue on that:

The Secret

What the Bleep Do We Know?

Fahrenheit 9/11

The Fog of War

In each case we follow a "hero" and like all stories, these too are about "transformation." In this case, in addition to the hero, we are the ones transformed by new information, and in our "All Is Lost" moment, the "whiff of death" is the death of an old idea.

The essence of all communication can be found in the BS2, and the basics of storytelling are the same, no matter what language we use to tell it, and no matter what form.

The struggle to get our stories out is the same whatever canvas we use. Tell me a story. I love to find it, and understand it, and play with it, in every area of communication.

BOOM!... FADE OUT.
March 24, 2008

If you're looking for a nice family film you can actually show every demographic in your household, I would point you to *August Rush*. I saw it Friday with my actual family (not one I appear with on TV) and we never had to look away once in fear that something untoward would pop up. It was a very sweet little movie with a nice message and you'll recognize the singers who appear in the church scene from the Oscar* awards this year.

What *August Rush* has too is a big finish. It's one of those endings that we lead up to throughout the film with everything coming together in the final emotional climax. It feels like the writers pinned a lot of hope on this culminating moment, and it may not be entirely successful. Oddly, nothing really happens in *August Rush*, no one changes, really, and it may have been in service of trying to make the ending powerful.

Not to give too much away, but the movie centers on a musically-gifted child separated from his parents who hopes to bring them together — and does (and no I'm not giving anything away by telling you that!). The whole script is geared to the last moment, that one last look in the eyes of the principals, that one last explanation for why we came, and then we pretty much go to black.

It peaks in the final scene, and then it ends.

I don't know if it was written this way, if the writers found the ending as they went, or started out thinking "wouldn't it be cool to have it all conclude in the last minute!" from the very beginning. But it's an interesting movie convention that I love to see attempted and don't see often enough.

And it got me thinking that this story capper almost belongs in its own category because it offers such unique challenges.

The big finish, the one we've been waiting for throughout the film, and go out on once seen, is an art, and one of the great pleasures of being a movie watcher. As a screenwriter, I have never tried this, probably because it is usually more geared to dramas and thrillers.

Of the great endings like this, I can think of a couple that truly took my breath away.

#1 on my hit parade for the most shocking, abrupt — and yet still satisfying — ending ever is Alfred Hitchcock's *Vertigo*. The final moment in which Jimmy Stewart, and we, realize what's happened and the fact this mystery really is over, literally stunned me. I saw this movie on VHS when the re-issue first came out and I could have sworn they cut out a part. But no. It's just one of the great endings of all time.

Another would have to be the original *Shop Around the Corner*, also a Jimmy Stewart starrer, this one a romantic comedy and one Nora Ephron based *You've Got Mail* on. The original ends with the reveal that Margaret Sullavan now knows who her pen pal lover is, and that he's staring her right in the face with the telltale flower in his lapel signifying his secret admirer status. We've been waiting the whole movie for this moment, to see the lovers reveal themselves to each other. And as I recall, it's the last thing we see. Fade out.

The art of running up to and executing the big finish is one I would like to try in future scripts, and in fact the challenge of figuring out the best, most shocking, most spectacular Boom!... then Fade Out, might be a great starting point for a screenplay you write.

Meantime, what are your all-time, great final scenes that immediately go to THE END?

There's always this one that I use to end many a phone machine message:

"Oh, and by the way, I hid the gold in the..."

But that's really meant to make you call me back!

CHAPTER 7

July 21, 2009
*"To make a character pop, who he is must be reflected
in the way he talks."*

DIALOGUE

DIALOGUE CLINIC
July 21, 2009

Recently I've been asked to help screenwriters buff up their scene-writing skills and in particular those scenes in which characters and dialogue fail to inspire.

The critique comes back with things like "the dialogue is on the nose," "the scene is flat," or "all the characters talk the same."

So how do you address these complaints?

First off, I always start with structure. One of the reasons we roll out our classes like we do — going from vetting the logline and working out the 15 Beats in the first workshop, then moving to the 40 scenes of The Board in the second — is to make sure all the scenes are necessary. If we aren't moving the story forward, if we've somehow lost track of the "bouncing ball" that is your hero's transformation, maybe it doesn't belong at all?

But let's say for the sake of argument that the scene is worthy, but just a little limp. Now what?

My approach is to see every scene as a "module of drama." I like to say that every scene is a mini-story — complete with 15 Beats that show change. It's true! Start watching scenes in your favorite films and see how the 15 Beats show up — including the All Is Lost that shows a "death" about three quarters of the way in. Like any story, the scene hero has to have a tangible goal; what is that? And who or what is countering the hero? Finding motive reveals where the white-hot light of conflict is. If you have scenes where characters are "talking about what they're doing," it's time for a triage.

As to characters talking the same, man, I hate that. Part of my dilemma with working on scripts with flat characters is: I can't tell one character from another. And no, that's not the reader's fault; it's yours. To make a character pop, who he is must be reflected in the way he talks. Ten different people can walk in a room and say "Hi!" ten different ways, but it's all about revealing something about that character. If you're not sure if you have this problem, try the Bad Dialogue Test: Cover up the names of characters speaking and see if you can tell who's talking by the way he or she talks. It's key.

Finally, like everything else, it's about finding inspiration, and applying it. Listen to the way friends and strangers speak. Keep a notebook of "interesting things overheard at Starbucks" that will reveal how oddly we speak sometimes, and how what we say is merely cover for what we really mean in the subtext of what we say! Put that insight to work in your script, making the character come alive — even if it's someone we hate! I always find that the key to writing any story is to love ALL the characters, regardless of their deeds. By trying to understand them better, and making them enunciate who they are, flat scenes stand up strong.

A POT OF SPAGHETTI

January 11, 2007

I love story! And I love helping to fix problems in any story — it is my passion.

And in a sense what I love about it is — it's so do-able. Screenwriting is problem-solving. Putting a story out there and getting feedback to figure out where we missed the mark, or failed to communicate properly, is what the smart screenwriter does before sending that script out and having it land on Spielberg's desk.

Better to know now the condition of your dream project than when the phone rings and it's your buddy at Paramount with the results.

One problem that comes up a lot is character and dialogue. We all read scripts where the story is in place and the character voices aren't. I am working with one writer now whose story is superb but whose characters are "place-holders" at the moment, stand-ins for the real, juicy roles that actors want to play, with mouth-watering dialogue and great, perfect buttons!

So how do you get there from here?

My response to bland character and dialogue problems is this thought: What if this were a radio play? What if all you had at your disposal to tell your story was a microphone broadcasting to the public? I must admit this mental picture was nurtured by my start in show biz as a voice talent for my TV producer dad. I was pushed in front of a microphone to play the kid's parts in many of my dad's cartoons, surrounded by amazing adult voice talents such as Sterling Holloway (voice of *Winnie the Pooh*) and Gary Owens (who was *Roger Ramjet*)! I saw these great voice talents take the lines written for "Screwy Squirrel" or some other such animal character and turn them into... characters. By giving Screwy the voice of, say, Ronald Coleman or Kirk Douglas, that animated animal became a whole new being — and often altered the way that cartoon character would be written in future stories.

So here's what I recommend, especially if you are about to send your script out and want one last test to see if characters work. I call it the "Pot of Spaghetti Test." Step One: Make a pot of spaghetti. Step Two: Invite a bunch of thespians over to your house. Yes, you heard me! Actors, baby! Friends who like to emote, the more ebullient the better! Then after enjoying your spaghetti dinner... Step

Three: Have a reading. Divvy up the parts and get your extroverted friends to play around with their roles, try one voice, then another for each character, and get a feel for who these people on the page really are. Step Four: Record the reading. Only after everyone has gone home and you are cleaning spaghetti sauce off the walls (how did it get up THERE!?) should you replay the tape — even better the next morning. Step Five: Yes! Re-write accordingly.

My bet is your friends will give you clues that reveal what needs to be done with character, and that your script is so shockingly not ready to go out to anyone... at least not yet!

SAY HELLO TO MY LITTLE CLICHÉ!
August 13, 2007

I was doing something unusual the other day — watching TV. And while poking around the dial, I saw a promo for a show called *Psych*. Seems like a fun show, set in my hometown of Santa Barbara, CA, but I saw something that turned me off. There is the star of the show, and he is doing an imitation of Al Pacino in *Scarface*. "Say hello to my leetle frien'," says our hero and I thought, well, I guess I won't be watching this.

Why?

Because I have heard every variation on "Say hello to my little friend" there is. It's a joke and an imitation that should be retired.

But shame on me, because while going through an old script this weekend, I found something similar that made my hair curl.

"I won't do it," says my character stamping his foot. "You won't get me to do that in a million years. God as my witness, I will never put on a dress." CUT TO: The next scene, where, you guessed it, the character is wearing the dress. (It wasn't exactly that bad, but you get the point.)

We are talking about cliché, and our #1 job as screenwriters is to avoid these. These are old jokes, tired rhythms, lame parodies, and, yes, imitations of old movies we and our friends around the water cooler have seen a million times. It's time to dispense with them all.

CLICHÉ CONFLAGRATION
August 23, 2007

Over the course of my career, I have seen my share of bad puns, overused lines, tired camera angles, and well-worn jokes.

As screenwriters, our job is to make sure that anything we send out is the freshest, newest take, and one we have never seen before. This is the nature of our job. So don't be afraid of clichés, get to know them and learn to avoid them. If nothing else, use them as a springboard to find the take we have never heard or seen.

I myself have been guilty of the cliché. As a young writer it felt safer to use a joke others had used before me — wouldn't they like me too if I said it?

Now if I find myself using a dull witticism or someone else's joke, I either dump it or give it a twist that makes it new. Every aspect of our job is like that: Give me the fresh take on the rom-com, the ghost story, the epic adventure. Let me see the characters I have NEVER seen before with quirks and aspirations that make them new. Don't give me the outcome I expect, surprise me!

CLICHÉ ALERT!!
January 8, 2006

As stated repeatedly in *Save the Cat!*, the screenwriter's job is to constantly scour our writing looking for the cliché — and stomp it out. Whether it's the hackneyed idea, the dull turn of phrase, or the been-there-bored-by-that character, it's our duty to make everything about our screenplays — and our writing — POP!

And that means never settling for what is less than fresh and new.

I've just finished reviewing my usual 1000 words a day and found them laced with phrases like "when push comes to shove," "the be all and end all," and "don't go there." Ugh! But instead of beating myself up — for too long, anyway — I see these "place holders" for what they are: an opportunity to liven up my writing with a fresh way to say the same thing — by saying it *my* way.

What is your most common screenwriting cliché? Is it the FADE IN: that begins with a car chase, murder, or young girl running through a forest being pursued by some loudly breathing — but unseen — monster?

Is it the staid character that uses tired phrases in the attempt for the screenwriter to sound "hip" for "the kids" in the audience?

Odds are if it feels like you've seen it or heard it somewhere before, it's time to re-think and re-write. That comforting feeling that "It's like a movie, therefore it's safe for me to use it" is in fact misleading you into the world of Cliché Alert! And as they say in the now tired words from my writing today: Go there not!

THE DA VINCI EXPOSITION
May 21, 2006

In *Save the Cat!*[*] I write about Basil Exposition, the character from Mike Meyers's *Austin Powers* series played by Michael York. Basil is an inside joke, especially his last name, because every time he appears onscreen that's all he does: Give the exposition. Basil tells Austin, and us, the history, state of, and future of the case that Meyers' British superspy is trying to solve. And everyone, even Austin, rolls his eyes whenever Basil appears.

Imagine a whole movie peopled by no one but Basil Exposition!

Ron Howard's *The Da Vinci Code* is a good, solid, entertaining movie. I don't buy the backlash by critics who dub it a disaster. For fans of the book, the tale is enhanced by the visuals and settings. And Tom Hanks gives a truly weird performance that is definitely worthy of a look.

But!

Man, what an exposition headache!

While watching the film last night (a packed house by the way), all I heard was characters talking the plot. And when they weren't talking the plot, they were flashing back to scenes from history — and personal backstory — that gave me whiplash.

I advise screenwriters to try to avoid the flashback and the dream sequence and this movie will give me lots of headaches when writers say: "They did it in *The Da Vinci Code*!"

I am a big Akiva Goldsman fan, the screenwriter who adapted Dan Brown's book, but I sensed the struggle. Every character was forced to talk. And talk. And talk. And all the talk — or 90% of it — had to do with events that were not occurring in the present. Only occasionally did drama get in the way of "facts."

It made me realize why there was such controversy about Dan Brown adapting so much of his fictional work from the purely historical speculation found in books like *Holy Blood, Holy Grail*. Because of the nature of screenwriting versus a narrator telling a tale to us in a book, it reveals how much of Brown's work is really just based on this outlandish conspiracy theory. Perhaps this story is not really a story at all but a documentary?

Also, try though they might to give Tom, as hero Robert Langdon, a "limp and an eye patch" — that being his having a life-altering trauma as a child — there was no "arc" in Tom's character. Yes, they hurtled across France and England finding clues and avoiding bad guys, but nothing *happened*. Not really. Or not enough to transform Tom's character anyway.

And that is what a really good story is about.

After all, Basil Exposition is the same in the first *Austin Powers* movie as the last. When the only purpose of a character is to function as a plot teller, there really isn't much room for more.

"I... DRINK... YOUR... MILKSHAKE!"
February 7, 2008

We are writers, aren't we?

Why yes, by God we are, Blake!

And it is our business, is it not, to be interested in those lines of dialogue from movies and TV that stick in the minds of our audience, even to the point where they become part of the culture?

They call them "catch phrases" around the offices of *Saturday Night Live*, and some TV writers, like those who work on that late night comedy show, try hard to coin them.

In screenwriting, we like coming up with them too, but only occasionally are these planned.

There is a whole passel from those Arnold Schwarzenegger *mooofies*, when Arnold, say, dispatches a bad guy by dowsing him in gasoline and lighting a match, then casually notes: "What a hothead."

I can't imagine "I... Drink... Your... Milkshake!" the ultimate, frightening, all-powerful line delivered by Daniel Day-Lewis in *There Will Be Blood* was meant to be one of these, but it is now.

This is from the scene where Daniel reveals to his final foe how he tricked him, explaining that the land his enemy thought was safe from Daniel's oil drilling was accessible via an adjoining tract. Like having a straw long enough to drink another fella's milkshake. Screenwriter Paul Thomas Anderson took the line straight out of congressional testimony from the Tea Pot Dome Scandal in the 1920s.

And it makes for dramatic testimony of its own in the final scene of his Academy Award®-nominated film.

I now find myself saying "I... Drink... Your... Milkshake!" every chance I get.

I hang around McDonald's looking for an excuse to say it, spooking little kids, who think I actually want their milkshake. They don't know who Daniel Day-Lewis is.

Or why his name is hyphenated.

"I... Drink... Your... Darjeleen!" I say while killing time at Coffee Bean and Tea Leaf. Startled customers call the manager over to complain.

"Oh that guy," he tells them. "He's always in here pitching movie ideas."

And it's so much better than when I used to loiter near the ATM in the early '90s saying: "Go ahead. Make my day."

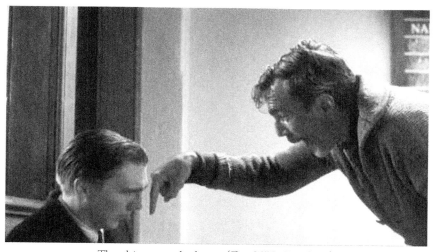

The ultimate catch phrase. (*There Will Be Blood* 2007)

Yup. There Will Be Blood, people.

There Will Be Lunch.

There Will Be Dinner.

And later? There Will Be Snacks.

Do you think I am too into this movie?

CHAPTER 8

February 9, 2009
"Pitch, is all I'm saying.
Put your movie idea into a form you can tell others about...
and get them interested."

THE PITCH

HINTS FOR PITCHING
July 2, 2007

The pitch is not the most important thing a writer will do, writing is, but we are all called upon to describe our movie — and to do so in the pithiest way we can.

I lay out four things I think every good logline should have in *Save the Cat!* I also talk about the importance of including adjectives to describe the players of your movie. I need to see a "type" of protagonist and a "type" of antagonist, in addition to the conflict between them. Saying your hero is a "wannabe" actor or a "disgraced" cop or a "childless" couple — and doing the same for your antagonist — is key. It gives the listener a handle on who they should root for, a mind picture of the situation you are describing.

But here is the best tip for pitching, and one that ties directly into story:

In "beating out" any story, I suggest using the 15 Beats of the Blake Snyder Beat Sheet. It is the foundation upon which all good stories can be built. One of those 15 beats I call the "Fun and Games." It's the section just after the Break into Act Two, when the hero first lands in the "upside-down version of the world" that will be the setting for the bulk of the story.

The "Fun and Games" section is where we see "the promise of the premise" — and the "poster." When tomboy FBI agent Sandra Bullock first goes undercover at a beauty pageant in *Miss Congeniality*, the "Fun and Games" section is when she gets her makeover, and awkwardly teeters on her high heels. This is when Sandra first lands in "Girl World" and is overwhelmed by having to wear that sash, and wave politely, and learn to do her musical water glass talent.

Well, guess what? Look at the "one-sheet" of *Miss Congeniality*. There's Sandra with her ball gown, and her sash, and strapped to her thigh — her gun. It's the poster of the movie.

It's also the pitch.

Fun and Games is the pitch of every movie. It's the shank of your movie idea, the place in the script where I can best see "What is it?" So if you are trying to get a handle on what your movie idea is in order to pitch it, look to the Fun and Games section on your beat sheet. The Fun and Games is not only where we find the most "trailer moments," it is the essence of what your movie is about.

The writers I send off to pitch all have success thinking of their movie in this way. It helps them figure out exactly what their story is!

SOLVING THE PUZZLE
June 23, 2008

This year's Great American Pitchfest was terrific.

I loved, loved, loved the time I had meeting with all the writers in attendance.

I got to test out some new theories on how to "turn out" your movie idea, how to find the "grabber" of it — and by doing so not just have a better pitch but a better story! Storytelling gets simpler the more you exercise your skills, that's the good news. When I hear a pitch — and hear a problem in it — the fix is usually easy. There are basic things that misfire, and those are usually just a matter of adjustment.

Blake with his good friend Signe Olynyk of the Great American Pitchfest.

But the hurdle is what it's always been for creative people. Can you let go of your preconceived notion of what it is, and hear what listeners are telling you? And if you keep getting the same rejection over and over, can you huddle in your creative place and come back out with the solution?

This, to me, is what it's all about. Story is a puzzle. And getting all the pieces to fit just right is not just a good sales tool, it's the point of the job. The challenge also has to be fun!

Here are some things found in the pitches that don't work:

— An idea that's a gimmick, not a story

— A hero with no goal and no obstacle in the way

— Concepts that are too simple, or flat when you hear them and...

— Confusion of ideas. A confusing idea is like a Chicken Omelette; you can't quite put your finger on exactly what's wrong — but there's something about the concept that just isn't right!

I thank all the writers I met this weekend for your love and support. I wish you all real success in the world and think about you every day hoping that today you will have the breakthrough that changes your lives!

The Great American PitchFest – Speaker Evaluation
SAVE THE CAT WITH BLAKE SNYDER

Please take a moment to provide feedback on this session so that we can continue to improve your PitchFest experience.

Please rate the SPEAKER(S) in each of the following areas:

	Poor	Fair	Good	Excellent
Knowledge of Subject Material				✓
Delivery of their Message				✓
Ability to Answer Questions				✓
Overall Rating for This Speaker				✓

Comments: _Exceptional_

WHEN IS "GOOD FOR YOU" BAD?
January 15, 2009

I recently got an email pitch from a writer asking for my opinion.

I may not have given the response he wanted to hear, but I've heard so many pitches lately that have hit me the same way, I wanted to point out something you may be doing, too.

The movie pitched to me was what I like to think of as "good for you." The basis of the pitch was that this film has deep meaning, and if you watched it you'd learn something and be better for it.

Well, as admirable as that is... it's not the way to pitch.

We all should have good intentions as writers, and when we find our theme, and the "moral of the story," it's a great day! As I've stated many times, every story we tell has to be "about something"; it has to have meaning beyond the surface story, and we have to have a desire to tell it beyond mere commerce — and finding that meaning is vital, whether we begin writing with it in mind or discover it along the way.

But that's the B Story. That's the Theme. That's the Spiritual Goal of the hero(es). It's the "underneath story."

The A Story is what lures us in to say "send me that script" or to buy a ticket to see your well-intentioned movie. And the crux of every pitch is the "Fun and Games" section of the script. When the hero crosses into Act Two, and enters the "upside-down version of the world" — that's the concept, that's the poster.

That's your pitch.

Don't pitch me your good intentions. I assume I will be edified and empowered by your tale — if you follow the *Cat!* method, your story will resonate with meaning found in how the hero is transformed. But it's a "spoonful of sugar" that helps the medicine go down.

Draw me into your good intentions with an idea that intrigues, and you have a much better chance to enlighten me as I walk out of the theater at the movie's end, thinking:

What a meaningful movie!

ICEBERG! ICEBERG!

May 18, 2009

My Mom, God love her! She is my idol! A stock market genius! The most tasteful, brilliant, and insightful person I've ever known, and the one person whose opinion I really trust.

But she can't pitch a movie to save her coupons.

One of the reasons for this is how she comes at telling a story. Getting to "what's it about?" is often a long road. And as her patient son, I often must wait for the punchline.

As I now tell audiences all over the world (having gotten permission from my Mom), this is how she would break the news of the Titanic sinking...

"You know the Astors," she would begin.

Yes.

"Well, they're having marital problems, so they go on vacation in France..."

Yes...

"And they decide to come home, so they book passage on this wonderful ship..."

Yes!?

"And everyone on board is so nice to them, all their friends are there too...."

YES!!??!

By the time we get to the part that's the headline of the story, I am at wit's end trying to figure out what she's trying to tell me... and by the time she gets to the part about the ship hitting the iceberg, I'm confused by all the details. Mom falls into a storytelling no-no we all must fight, called "burying the lead."

Iceberg! Iceberg! Mom I want to say. Get to the part that's the reason you're telling this story.

I bring this up because I hear a lot of movie pitches that fall into this category, too. What is it? I want to ask. Tell me the headline! I want to know. So get to the point! Pleeeeeezzzeee. And for friends of mine who've heard me tell the story of my Mom and the Titanic, I now say: *Iceberg! Iceberg!*

It's a little reminder to get us all to the point.

Are you pitching your movie like my dear, sweet Mom? Are you telling us details up front that aren't germane to the essence of the story, and avoiding the headline, the grabber that makes us stay interested? If so, before you go into that pitch meeting or agent confab, think of my Mom, and remember:

Iceberg! Iceberg!!

Mom can tell me the story any way she wants to, by the way! So these days when she says "Did you hear about the_____," I just smile, grab a seat, and listen to every detail. I love you, Mom!!

WHY I HARP ON CONCEPT
February 9, 2009

One of the many disciplines *Save the Cat!* endorses is the cultivation and clear enunciation of your ideas.

It's not enough to be inspired, it's not enough to "see" your movie.

Can you get someone *else* to see it, too?

Screenplays are blueprints for further action. And action starts with the idea.

If you can get yours into a form I find intriguing, I will ask to see that script.

If the script is well told (and that means well-structured, another *STC!* principle), I as producer will ask: Who is this for? And can it be made and released for a price that will make back an investment?

And finally, once I've asked for your script, bought it, and made it into a movie, I now have to tell others about it, and tell your idea a third time in a smart advertising campaign. It's a $30 – $50 million investment in P & A (prints and advertising) on average for the typical major studio release.

But just because we're "only the writer" doesn't mean this information cannot inform what we do, too.

Pitch, is all I'm saying. Put your movie idea into a form you can tell others about... and get them interested. Whether it's a lively poster line that sums up your movie in a catchy slogan; a tight logline that hints at the beginning, middle, and end of your hero's adventure; or a treatment that grabs our attention — grab it! Not only will you have a better chance of selling your project, but the discipline of clearly stating what your movie is about will make the writing of that story that much better, too!

THE "DEATH" OF HIGH CONCEPT
February 2, 2006

Every once in a while we aspiring screenwriters question our methods. If Hollywood is making a lot of "high concept" movies that fail, is the high concept movie dead? And in a world that is changing, where movies might soon be seen on iPods instead of in big-screen theaters, does that mean storytelling has to change too?

In the past few days I realized once again why the basics still apply and why no matter what the delivery system may be, the rules of writing stories that satisfy still hold.

This past weekend we saw Steven Soderbergh's *Bubble* premiere. It's a movie that will be best known as the first to be released in theaters and as a DVD on the same day. But the manner of distribution doesn't matter if no one wants to see the movie — and *Bubble* has barely made a ripple.

I also got a lesson in sticking to my guns while out pitching this week. For as poorly as the typical "Hollywood" movie is perceived in any given year, the rules of why the good ones work still hold.

Having a pitch that is easy to describe is still the coin of the realm in Hollywood and my studio meetings this week confirmed this — again! My pitch to an executive must be translated to the studio head and, if we're lucky, eventually pitched to moviegoers. Across the board the test is the same: Am I interested in this idea or not? The old saw still applies: Does it grab me? If not, no sale.

Your movie idea must follow the rules, too. The so called "death" of high concept is better understood as the hoped-for death of bad movies. And the way to test to see if your ideas are good or bad is the same as everyone else's: Pitch someone. No matter how we get our ideas to an audience, you can't get past having to come up with one that doesn't make our eyes glaze over — whether in person, on your iPod, or on 3,000 screens.

ACT ZERO
March 11, 2009

I got a call from a well-known screenwriter the other day.

I get emergency phone calls like X's all the time to make sure they have their pitch straight, often just hours before going into their meeting.

I got these calls before *Save the Cat!*® of course.

But now I get them a lot.

X was rarin' to go! Coffee-ed up, he jumped right in. X had 10 minutes of material — all great — about where the hero was born, where he went to school, what key moment in his life caused him to be him....

And then the movie starts, I said, kind of hoping X would get the point.

No. Not yet. Because X had more!

More back story. More pipe. More explanation.

And then the movie starts, I said, more insistently.

About three objections in, it finally dawned on the pitcher.

That was the pitch.

That was the movie.

And yet nothing happens, I said.

Silence. I could hear the wheels turning in the writer's head. All that great set-up, all those great details about what kind of clothes the hero wore, where he went to school, all that stuff meant nothing....

... at least to an audience.

Panic. Now what? X didn't have anything. But with a little work cutting stuff we didn't need, and getting the story started without it, we found not only where the movie began, but how to get a better grasp on everything after it starts: theme, meaning, resonance, and a finale that matched the opening.

Will all that character work go to waste? Not at all. But we can put it all in a new act that one writer suggested I call "Act Zero." The stuff we need to know BEFORE the movie starts... that no one else really wants to hear.

"Tell me a story" means fewer adjectives and adverbs and more verbs and nouns. Verbs are especially good. But when it comes to writing backstory and character biography, to me that has to come out "on the fly" and "on the run" as the story unfolds — and only about a tenth of it, or less, will ever be actually used.

It will still be on the page, and in the character... not just as blatantly as one might think!

A more pleasant phone call came later that day: The writer got the job! He had figured out how to tell the story without burdening his audience with backstory. The writer had gotten to the heart of the plot quicker and slicker.

Your imagination is a powerful thing. It paints pictures like crazy — and a lot of the painting is absolutely necessary. But we have to be editors, too. Deciding what is important in any story we tell — no matter how we tell it — is the job. And just because we're dazzled by the details doesn't mean others will be too.

Try putting all that backstory into the place we'll never see it, in the Act before the Action starts: Act Zero.

THEATER OF THE MIND
January 26, 2009

Lately I've really enjoyed working with writers via phone.

Usually a script question can be answered easily in an email, but sometimes it's better to talk.

A few of these conversations are with well-known screenwriters, which proves even the pros need perspective.

They are about to go into a meeting, and just want to double-check with me about a pitch point or a story hiccup. I fielded these emergency calls long before *Save the Cat!* came out, but even more so since.

And I love it.

Because no matter who is calling, or what story they're working on, every conversation is different. And I'm the one who always learns something new.

Tell me your story I will say. A breath. Okay. And with a little nudging from me about what I really need to hear — and what I don't — the cavern of my imagination lights up with their story. A flare set off in a diamond mine. And in quick order, the flaws appear, too. A long list of things can be the cause:

— Characters that aren't arcing... or aren't there!

— Third acts that fail to pay off what was promised up front.. and maybe it's what's up front that's off?

— Midpoints that blur... because the writer has not decided whether it's a "false victory" or a "false defeat."

And often it's like therapy. Because that fatal story flaw, the section that "needs some work" is staring the writer in the face, and he hasn't come to grips with what the real "work" is.

I feel like a radio psychologist, because inevitably the problem is a blind spot the writer has, or some nagging reality he's known about from the start, and is trying to pave over with dazzle. But it all comes out in our talk. And often it doesn't take long before we have a much firmer grasp of the poster, the hero, the death of the hero's old ideas, and the final test he must pass. Or not.

It's amazing how vivid a picture can be painted with a few words — if those words are well-chosen. And if the right questions are asked, and you have the flexibility to think a new way, these stories can be re-booted many times until you get it right.

But have no doubt this is the process. Before we commit to a real theater, or a real movie set, we first have to put our story up in the Theater of the Mind. Whether you tell me or your writer's group, or the stranger in line at Starbucks, the more you do, the better you get at it — so the umpteenth time you tell it is the right way.

And when it is finally committed to a bigger stage, with people you've never met responding to your story, it will still be the story they will be able to tell each other, to urge everyone *they* tell to see the most amazing thing they've ever seen. What is that? How does it go? A breath. Okay.

It goes something like this...

CHAPTER 9

March 3, 2009
"I wanted something I could DO immediately
that would resonate not only with audiences, but with the gatekeepers
who separated me from the audience."

GOING PRO

SILLY LITTLE RULES
June 28, 2006

As a screenwriter in charge of my own destiny, I must survive by any means possible out here in movie land.

And part of that survival is: I have to know what the tea leaves say; I gotta know how I'm doing in a world full to the brim with invisible signals, unspoken truths, and a sophistication of symbols worthy of a geisha and her fan. Every gesture tells a story! But what are the gestures telling me?

So once I send my script out, pitch my story, or go in to the studio to make a sale and am waiting for an answer, how do I know how I am doing?

Here are some of my silly little rules that help me cope:

1. All Good News Happens Before Noon! I don't know why this is, but it is. Whenever I am waiting for an answer, I only have to wait until 1:00 p.m. If the phone hasn't rung by the time they've gone to lunch — it's a "no."

2. Two Weeks Is Too Long. If you are still reading my script two weeks from now and have not called me, you are not interested. I don't get mad, I don't get upset, but I do get on with my life.

3. "We'll talk about this among ourselves and get back to you." If you hear this statement by a studio executive after you have gone in to his/her office and pitched your movie idea, this is a "pass" — even if it's accompanied by "It's great!", "We love it!", or "We want to be in business with you."

(And by the way, God bless 'em! What else can they say? It's so much nicer than being thrown out with: "And never darken our towels again!!!")

4. The sudden doctor's appointment. Picture this: You are on your way to the meeting, you have prepared your pitch, you've sweated bullets all night getting ready — and your cell phone rings: The exec is canceling! He's gone to the doctor. No, he hasn't.

5. Silence Is Not Golden. When you have gone in to pitch your idea, and they say they'll call back but they don't, and seasons change, and you're still waiting to hear, well, you have heard.

6. "As soon as we get back from Cannes..." aka "As soon as we get back from Telluride..." aka "As soon as we get back from lunch..." They never come back. Say goodbye and God love ya! And thanks for the Evian!

7. "We have something like that in development" = "Good idea!"

8. "I loved your movie!" = "I just Imdb'd you."

9. "I just have to check with my partner." (see Rule 6)

10. "I'll call Business Affairs. Would you like them to call your agent or your manager?" Congratulations! You can now reassess Rules 1-9.

All of this, of course, is about the most important thing: moving forward. When I get hung up waiting for someone else, odds are I'm not doing what I've been put on this earth to do: write! The tyranny of not knowing is mostly what it does to my spirit — and my attitude. Well, forget it, and get back to work. Write, query six new potential buyers, make contacts, help others. That takes my mind off the things that are out of my control, and back onto the fun of doing this job. And that's what it's really about.

A QUESTION
October 27, 2008

"It seems very difficult to find an agent or agency to even look at one of my scripts. Other than query letters and phone calls is there any other way to find someone to represent me?"

I say this to writers all the time, and will address it in the future, but believe it or not, finding an agent is not the most important thing on your to-do list. The most important thing is writing a great screenplay. If you build it, they will come — and that's a fact. But let's say you have your script in hand, it's vetted, you know it's great, and you're ready to begin marketing it. What then?

1. I do recommend query letters and email queries. They work. But if you are not getting 4-10 responses for every 100 email or query letters you send — it's not the agent, it's your pitch! Either your idea is a non-starter or the way you're telling it is; this is one reason I am so big on this blog about logline exercises.

2. Seek a manager instead of an agent. A manager is very often what I call a "stealth producer." In addition to representing you, he or she wants to be attached to your project, which adds to their interest. I think looking for a manager first is a great plan. We are seeking "partners," and the right manager can be a helpful one.

3. Managers can help you seek other "attachments" that will help get your movie made, though you can seek these too: talent, financing, directors, special effects packages. All these add-ons to a project will give it more momentum so someone will more likely want to join... because no one likes to "go first."

4. Short film, trailer, poster, pr campaign — if there is an element in your script that might lend itself to building some buzz, by all means try it. Can you create separate products, fan sites, or a You-Tube short that will build curiosity? Can you, if yours is a true story, query newspapers and magazines to write a non-fiction piece about your subject to create interest? Perhaps even posting a teaser — 10 pages of your script — on your home site or writers group page.

5. Other routes like contests, film festivals, etc. are also good if easy or enjoyable for you. I recommend the Final Draft contest, the Nicholls Fellowship, and many of the pitchfests including The Great American Pitchfest — but don't go expecting them to whip out their checkbook and buy your script on the spot; this is about building contacts and resources beyond just today.

THE QUERY QUERY
November 7, 2008

I have received a ton of email lately about an important topic: the query letter.

Whether it's an email query or an actual letter sent via snail mail, should we bother sending them, and what actually do we send when we do? Well, the short answer is "Yes!" you should definitely send these out. But what actually do we put into those communiqués to elicit the best possible response?

One of my all-time favorite writers is Kathy Hepinstall, a successful novelist, and now a successful screenwriter with a very bright future. She wrote recently to offer her opinion on the subject:

I think it's extremely important how query letters are written. For example, when I was peddling my first novel, I sent around a query letter that began something like this:

Dear ____

I have written a literary novel, about 80,000 words, set in Louisiana in 1941, about a very peculiar bordello, run by men.... (blah blah blah)

Not a bad query letter. I got 10 percent response. Then I really started thinking about query letters. They are really small pieces of advertising. As such, they must get the agent's attention in the first sentence in the most compelling way possible, or you've lost them, because literary agents receive buckets full of query letters.

So I rewrote it. Second query letter began: What happens when a woman finds out her own rapist has been put in charge of her spiritual recovery?

Got triple the response rate from that query letter: 30 percent. From those responses, I sent my manuscript to a very respected agent, who sold my novel in three days. So that's the advice I'd offer — make the query letter as compelling as you can in the very first sentence.

Screenwriter Ben Frahm connected with his current representatives through email query; he got about 4 to 5 responses from over 100 he sent. It sounds like a small number, but he had a good hook. As a result of this and a lot of hard work, Ben sold *Dr. Sensitive* to Universal and Tom Shadyac last year in a spec sale.

Point is: it works.

THE TREATMENT
June 2, 2006

I have just received an email from a writer in NYC who has been hired to write a script. As part of the process she's been asked to deliver a treatment of the screenplay first.

But what is that?

Ah! The Treatment. This is the fabled under-10-page overview of the movie a writer may or may not get to execute, that will inspire, delight, and tickle the reader — and mostly convince he or she (usually a producer, investor, or studio exec) that this movie deserves to live. But what exactly should a treatment contain, and how can you write a better one?

Like anything at the initial stages of writing a script, the treatment should be thought of as a "sell piece."

It is short, atmospheric, and makes the reader want to see more, i.e., hire you to go on and write the script! But it is not a beat-for-beat description.

The reader cares less about how you are going to execute the nuts and bolts of the script itself; what the reader wants is to get a feeling of the experience of this movie. Yes, there is a beginning, middle, and end. But we care less about your act breaks than why this story should be told.

I have written "clever" treatments, sometimes using the theme of the movie as a springboard. I have also spent more time on the treatment than on the actual script. And that's a mistake.

The best treatments are good narratives, complete unto themselves, that leave a little something on the table which makes us want to see more.

THERE'S NO "I" IN TEAM: AND OTHER LESSONS IN PARTNERSHIP
October 11, 2007

I am lucky in that all my experiences with my writing partners have been outstanding. I dedicate both *Cat!* books to my better halves because without them I'd be nowhere *mon frere*, and everything I've learned, I learned from them. Here are some points about the joys and pitfalls of life in the ampersand (&) lane:

FORMING A TEAM

I have gotten into partnerships in many ways, but it's always about the same thing: the desire to create a better story than I can create on my own! I think it's important to admire your writing partner, and to find someone who's a better writer in some way than you are. Like in tennis, you always learn more from stronger players. And all my partners have been my better in some area; their strengths are my weaknesses and vice versa. This is how I got to work with the brilliant C. David Stephens, whose chops as a horror maven far exceeded mine — thanks to the expertise he gained writing the classic *Cabin by the Lake*.

Many ask about the business arrangement I recommend. In my experience, I have never had a formal agreement with any partner. I have always worked on a handshake basis, split it all 50/50.

DAY TO DAY

My best writing experiences have followed a daily routine and that holds true for partnerships as well. Either Colby Carr comes over to my house, or I go over to Howard Burkons' house, or I fly to Tracey Jackson's beach retreat in Sag Harbor, or Jim Haggin and I meet every day in his or my office in Santa Barbara. We keep banker's hours, do our work, then take breaks. Time away from each other is a good thing! In terms of the actual work, my best results have come from the "overwriting" process, meaning that he or I will write the rough draft of a scene, the other guy will come in and overwrite, and on and on until we get it right. We usually start each script blocking it out. And amazingly, some of the biggest breakthroughs have happened at lunch while we were taking a time-out from the morning session — this is how Colby Carr and I figured out the Mr. Macintosh device in *Blank Check*, over lunch at "The Eurotrash Cafe." Thanks Ute!

Blake's framed copy of his *Blank Check* poster.

LIFE AS AN AMPERSAND

I have always gotten into my partnerships liking the person I was about to work with, and I always came away from the partnerships the same way. My friendship with these folks is paramount, and I personally would rather not play than to have a knock-down-drag-out fight over a script, business point, or other disagreement. My motto has always been "It's just movies," and no quibble point is worth bad blood in my opinion. I've always felt a certain amount of pride connected with being part of a team. And there is a bunker mentality that helps me weather a storm better, knowing that a partner has my back. Usually, they are the only ones who, when we come out of a meeting and an executive has punctured our balloon, really understands why it hurts.

PARTNER ETIQUETTE

I'm serious about the "No I in Team" rule. That's one Colby Carr and I always stuck to and it really helps. We made it a rule never to say "When I wrote this scene..." or "When I came up with this idea..." — not only because it made our team look unharmonious, but it tended to make the other guy defensive about getting his "I" in the next sentence. We literally stuck to "we" every time we discussed our script in a meeting. This goes for gossip, too. There is nothing that worries me more than when a writer "off the record" downplays his partner or tells tales out of school. If you're in the partnership, be in it.

MISCELLANEOUS

On the credits of a movie, you may or may not know, there are two ways to link more than one writer. "Written by X AND Y" means that two separate writers took a whack at the script. "Written by X & Y" means it's a team, both artistically and business-wise. This also is how the WGA divvies up residual payments. An "&" indicates one entity. Thus Written by X AND Y & Z shows that X will get 50% of residuals and Y & Z will get the other 50%. Not a small point.

FINALLY

I recommend it! Partnerships are wonderful. Just make sure you enjoy it, don't fight tooth and nail over a plot point to the extent that actual blood is spilled, and like any relationship, try not to get mean in the heat of an argument or make it so personal that you can't take back what you said. But for me, there's magic in partnerships, 1 + 1 often = 100 and the joy of creating is that much more special when shared!

TYLER PERRY'S QUIET SUCCESS
September 29, 2008

As a screenwriter ever interested in the entrepreneurial spirit of our industry, I must confess admiration for Tyler Perry. Though his work is critically panned, his legion of fans is amazing, and loyal to a fault. And the list of his successes, including *Diary of a Mad Black Woman* and *Madea's Family Reunion*, is all of a type — easy, family humor with a positive message.

Perry writes, directs, produces, and stars in comedies — often in the role of a cross-dressing matron — and he has turned his corner of the Atlanta film industry into a powerhouse of success. His secret? What I always claim is the most important aspect of any venture: Tyler knows his target market and caters to it unabashedly.

Much of the success of these films stems from Perry's background in the church. Most of his projects begin as church plays. The bugs are worked out in front of and by the key demographic — church goers, primarily woman and families — who consistently show up at the cineplex, too.

Like the Marx Brothers, who took their stage plays on the road to test which jokes worked best before turning on the cameras, Perry has found a sweet spot both in his method and his target. And while he may not get the credit he deserves, his lesson for screenwriters and filmmakers is obvious: Know thy niche!

How few studios have a brand! When you say "Pixar," you are saying 4-quadrant family films and know what to expect. But more and more the niche marketing is left to individuals who deliver a "Judd Apatow film" or a "Quentin Tarantino movie," and may indicate a future where we are carving out smaller, targeted groups for our own films.

What's your target market? Be it the art house, 4 quadrant family, date movie, prestige film, YouTube Generation short or global marketplace Indie, knowing who you are writing for, and loving them enough to cater to them, is more important than ever.

WATCH YOUR WORDS
May 7, 2009

As screenwriters, the power of words becomes second nature. Because every word counts, picking just the right ones is our job; we know their over-use or under-use can make or break our scripts and pitches.

Whenever I send in a new script, I always do a "white space alert" — just taking a long view of every page of my script to see if there's too much black and not enough white. Big blocks of dialogue. Chunks of description. Excess wordiness. All of it has to go. Even a quick scan of every page can reveal lots.

The "reading draft" or the "sales draft" of a script is just that — accented on selling a reader unfamiliar with your story. It is more focused on the hero's tale, steering the reader to the essentials of the story (for now), and getting them onboard to see its potential with a target audience. Once you've sold that script, the breakdown of each shot becomes prep for the director, cinematographer, and line producer, so the "shooting draft" is a brand new animal. Even here, every word counts when 1/8 of a page can be a day's shoot.

When pitching, my best advice to many writers is: learn when to shut up! Once you've told your story, come to the end, done your

Fade Out, the temptation to meet silence in the room with further elucidation can be overwhelming... but fatal. If you really have said it all, why say more? Let the buyer jump into the breach.

Crickets be damned!

We must also watch our words in what we speak about our script, our representatives, and our fellow writers. The self-fulfilling prophesy of talking up one's agent or one's script speaks volumes about where we are in our careers. Down-and-out moods lead to grumbling — and vice versa. So why shouldn't positive talk lead to success, fulfillment, and willing into reality the gossamer of ideas in our minds? How many writers have I heard say "My script is perfect for _____," only to have that actor or director actually appear?

Lots. There is something powerful not only in our written words, but in our spoken words as well.

Use them wisely.

Old Testament Genesis begins not with the waving of a wand to create the Earth in seven days, but *saying*: "Let there be light." Words have power. We know better than anyone. Let's make sure our words are well chosen.

REMAKES, REDOS, AND BASED-ONS
December 15, 2008

The good news is: you've got a script assignment! The bad news is: it's based on a TV show from 30 years ago, or a movie that had an impact for its time but may be out of phase for today's audience, or it's a title, but not a story, that in and of itself isn't enough to sustain a whole movie. So how do you approach it?

The value of these films for Hollywood is obvious. This weekend's *The Day The Earth Stood Still* is the latest attempt to take a known title and update it and it premiered at #1. The value of a so-called "pre-sold franchise" is clear. Name recognition is the biggest hurdle; a known "What is it?" is the reason remakes and redos will continue to get remade and redone. So the question is: what if we get a similar opportunity?

What are our guides to help us make our re-imaginings winners?

Let's start with films based on TV series. Most agree *The Fugitive* starring Harrison Ford is a high watermark. Whether you knew the backstory or not, or cared about its homage to "the one-armed man," we were given everything we needed to cheer both the chased (Ford) and the chaser (Tommy Lee Jones). I liked *The Brady Bunch* for its tongue-in-cheek ability to make fun of itself. Its winning take is based on a "fish out of water" convention for which even the uninitiated could root. Other successful renderings — *Mission:Impossible*, *The Untouchables*, and *Addams Family* — started with convention and broke from it.

Remakes are another challenge. What can you improve on with *Bad News Bears*, *The Heartbreak Kid*, or *Charlie and the Chocolate Factory*? Is it wise to go to the hits, the classics, the well-known, or really smarter to go after misfires — famous but flawed — as the basis of a remake? Either way, the challenge is the same:

Find the story.

ASSAYING THE "TRUE-LIFE" SCREENPLAY
March 2, 2007

I am currently having fun working one-on-one with several screenwriters who are writing either a true-life or a based-on-true-events screenplay. These are the "adaptations" we sometimes write, and just like any other script, they follow the same rules. One thing all writers have to be mindful of, but especially those that are writing anything based on fact, is the painful requirement to kill their "darlings."

What are they?

William Faulkner said that "In writing you must kill your darlings." These are the little gems, the bits of *writage* you can see yourself talking about with Anthony Lane or Ebert & Roeper over cocktails at Cannes where they tell you how brilliant you are — but in fact the darlings don't do anything to help the story. In biography, in true-life, in historic adaptation, the urge to keep the darling is more severe. "But it really happened!" you tell me. And it is my painful duty to tell you: So what? Poof! There goes your witty banter on the red carpet at the Oscars. Sorry! Hate to burst your bubble. But that's what's gotta happen.

Don't we all think of William Goldman, who wrote in *Adventures in the Screen Trade* about attempting again and again to put that "true life" scene of Butch Cassidy in as his opener of *Butch Cassidy and the Sundance Kid*? Try as he might, as good as it was, and as true as it was, it didn't work. So out it went. And often it is MY painful duty to tell writers that the whole biography is bad. Ouch!

As I like to point out, look at the movie *Alexander*. How is it possible that a guy with the most amazing feats of accomplishment in the history of mankind makes for such bad movies? They've tried it twice now, the latest directed by Oliver Stone, and each time... nada. Why? Maybe because Alexander's isn't a very good story? Because really what is it? He conquers Persia, he conquers India, he conquers Asia, The End. Sad, I know! It seems impossible, I know. But many times I must point out how the biography you are working on falls into the Alexander category. Just because it happened doesn't make it interesting. As history, fascinating! As story, a snooze.

And yet there are always ways to tell any story in a compelling fashion — as long as we are willing to get rid of our darlings, or in some cases, the darling that is our approach to the project as a whole.

We are storytellers. And as we know: All stories are about transformation. Tell me a story about a guy or gal who... transforms, and how that transformation affects those around him or her. When we lay out that story we ask: What does the hero want, and what's stopping him from getting it? And anything that doesn't attach itself to the spine of that story must come out.

If you don't have the pieces to make the connections in a "true-life" piece.... make them up! For in fact the opposite rule holds as well — the *Beautiful Mind* Rule which says that it's okay to whitewash, fuse together two or more characters into one, change locations of events, and even alter facts to make the story work. Yes, it drives historians batty. Yes, you may get flack from critics. But we must serve the story first. And so long as we are in sync with the spirit of the truth, and don't create anachronisms or falsehoods in the process, it's fair game.

I encourage you all to try this form at one point or another in your careers. The darling-killing muscle this exercises will become most useful when you return to the pure fiction of making up stories from scratch. Now when I tell you that the brilliant scene you came up with for your fictional cast of characters doesn't work, you may be less inclined to cling to it, and more inclined to serve the story first.

I-C-3-D!
April 3, 2009

Lunch with my favorite producer, Sheila Taylor, last Friday. Sheila is not only a great friend, and the author of the Forewords for the *Save the Cat!* books, but when she's not being the world's coolest person, she makes movies.

Sheila and her producing partners at Practical Pictures are currently working on *Final Destination 4* and have been in post-production for a year. One reason is this installment has something its predecessors didn't: 3-D.

3-D will give this amazingly successful franchise an extra dimension, and introduce it to a brand new audience, but the experience in 3-D filmmaking has been an exciting education for all involved.

3-D is not new, but adding to the sizzling box office with something extra is a recent surprise for the film business. Both *Monsters vs. Aliens* and *Coraline* got a financial boost thanks to this special effect, and while audiences don't have to see the movie in 3-D, having a higher ticket price for 3-D movies is a boon.

But what does 3-D mean for screenwriters? Should we be devising scenes with a hero flinging a yoyo right — *at!* — us or figuring out new ways for our slasher movies to splatter — *out!* — toward an audience?

Not every movie deserves 3-D treatment, of course, but if your movie has action, a fantasy world, or a horror element, thinking 3-D might not be bad. And while the traditional means of using 3-D still hold, often as a wink at the audience as they are — *attacked!* — by random objects coming at them, as Sheila explained, it's the sense of depth, and of a "world" that vanishes back into the screen that's really new.

There are several tiers of 3-D experimentation, but all offer new creative challenges. On the high end, both James Cameron and Bob Zemeckis have tied the technique to narrative, and their effect houses are considered the best. At a mid-range, adding in 3-D to a movie might not add that much cost. And even a combination of 3-D effects and computer animation makes for some really great thrills in *My Bloody Valentine*, which proved this year that the traditional scare effects 3-D is known for really do add to the experience.

On the set, 3-D playback is now possible thanks to a movable truck/ theater that can instantly let filmmakers view footage and go back for re-takes if the 3-D effect isn't all it can be. A full-on 3-D "Video

Village" is yet to be available, but with the boom in 3-D production, it will probably be in the offing soon.

For we screenwriters, the idea of just nailing down a story is challenge enough, and maybe the actual necessity of 3-D enhancement is best left to producers and studios. But given the technical boons available, and the demand of the marketplace, we must always be looking for ways to write to the technology, too. I personally have a whole new way to think of my family comedies coming — *at!* — my writer's group soon!

LIVE FROM AUSTIN!
March 12, 2007

I am in Austin, TX, at the South X Southwest Festival for one more day and the weekend has been great. We did a fantastic screenwriting panel this Saturday, talking about the future of the film business for writers. I am such a big believer in do-it-yourself. Entrepreneurial spirit is what it's all about — and always has been in the film business. When that spirit meets new technology, amazing things can happen.

The South X Southwest Festival started as a music festival, and music is still its biggest component. Later in the week the music portion of the gathering will get underway, but the initial section is devoted to film and interactive worlds. And the combining of the two makes sense. As Indie filmmakers reach out to promote their work, the use of the Internet goes beyond just spreading awareness of one's project.

One panel I got a chance to catch was the "Lonelygirl 15" creators. These are three smart guys from L.A. who decided to use YouTube to create a hoax — the fictional web cam diary of a girl that immediately became a sensation when viewers tried to guess whether she was real or not. When the hoax was revealed, the guys kept going, launching what is now a "Lost"-like web series that is driven as much by its viewers as its creators. Half game/half David Lynch soap opera, the show is supercharged by the fans who create their own videos to support the show —and even create new characters that spider out from the ones that exist. And the response is overwhelming: 1 million viewers a week and amazing fan loyalty. It is a show that got the creators representation, numerous offers to create TV series by the major networks, and film deals, including the eventual movie version of the series.

These guys do what we have been talking about all along, stressing the importance of knowing the basics of storytelling. This includes GETTING ATTENTION. This is what creating a great logline and poster for your movie is all about. In a future where there will be more product not less for audiences to choose from, how are you going to make your project stand out? Even when we choose not to write a film for the major studios, to go outside the system to write and make our projects, the basic rules are the same! Why should we watch your movie? But as the Lonelygirl 15 group proved, there is always a new way.

There are more opportunities for writers and filmmakers than ever before. But the rules are what they always have been: Get my attention, tell me a compelling, primal story. That and be open to all the tools available as a storyteller.

DIY

January 22, 2009

Do It Yourself.

That's what DIY stands for.

For screenwriters and filmmakers, DIY is about creating memorable short films that show off your storytelling skills.

But can a short, even one as brief as a minute or two, still hit the winning elements found in *Save the Cat!*"?

Of course it can!

In class, and in my new book, *Save the Cat!* *Strikes Back*, I talk about the 15 beats found in a 30-second commercial for Pledge furniture wax. And yes, it hits them all — including the "All Is Lost" beat when our housewife/hero confronts the "death of old ideas" as she drops her former polish product, Brand X, in the trash. This leaves her and Pledge to have a triumphant Finale as she walks out the door of her formerly messy house, dressed for tennis. That's a lot of transformation in 30 seconds!

The short, and very popular, YouTube hit, "Christian the Lion," and to an extent "The History of Dance," have these moments too. In fact, any YouTube short that relies on a story arc has a better chance to be popular if the creators follow the simple beats of "The Transformation Machine" that is good storytelling.

Key among these points, I'm finding more and more, is ID-ing the "All Is Lost" point. The "death" that must occur for your hero — either death of old ideas, realization of a defect of character, or sudden moment of clarity where there is no choice but to change — is key to every story, no matter its length.

This moment can even be spotted in *scenes*. It is now my habit to look for the "death moment" about three quarters of a way into any well-executed scene to find that thing that this scene is really about: change.

What YouTube shorts have you seen that "hit the beats" and reveal good storytelling? Odds are the ones you like best do so naturally. For all of us who approach DIY projects to create stories that resonate, the beats are a must to consider!

READ ANY GOOD SCREENPLAYS LATELY?

January 4, 2007

During the course of my speaking engagement in Chicago this past fall, I met with several writers working on great screenplay ideas. In talking to them about their scripts, I referenced certain movies I thought would be helpful. I also suggested they read the scripts for these movies. They hadn't read them; in fact, they told me, they rarely read screenplays.

No harm done, we can't be on top of every detail — I'm not — but it does suggest some further homework: What screenplays have you read lately?

I devoured the script of *Little Miss Sunshine* and really learned a lot. Michael Arndt, the author of *Sunshine*, has a great style of writing. It's clear, funny... and inspiring! Seeing the words on the page, and knowing the film, reminds me that it's possible to see our visions on screen (this was his first sale!!). And I learned a few tricks from his method of getting information across to readers, moving characters efficiently in and out of rooms, and voice! It's a fantastic example of how, on the page, every character is clear, distinct, and unique... just in the words they speak, a point I am forever preaching. And the movie itself is an example of what I have been suggesting we write for over a year, and what I think is still the "silver bullet" in screenwriting right now: high concept-low budget. In my opinion, that is the ticket to many more chances to sell your script.

So on your list of things to do this year, for yourself or your writing group, put down "read more scripts." If you're in a writing group, you might all read the same script as a group assignment and discuss what you learned.

Reading also will help you visualize how your award-winning screenplay will look... and get sold... and get made!

WELL-ROUNDED

July 2, 2009

Have you listened to *Rick Dees' Top Forty* lately?

What's the latest trend in Art?

Quick. Who's Frank Gehry?

If this sounds far afield from the subject of screenwriting, not so.

The topic is: being well-rounded. And it's a must for any writer attempting in his work of fiction to be current with "the news of the day." Being well-rounded is one of the great pleasures of our profession — and a great excuse for anyone asking why we're interested in any subject.

I'm a writer. I need to be up-to-date.

What are the latest trends in Art, Architecture, Pop Music, International Diplomacy, Science, and Astronomy? Who are the leaders at the cutting edge of Poetry, Medicine, History, Fashion, and Interior Design?

There is nothing worse when reading a script than finding an outdated pop culture reference, or sensing that this writer isn't up-to-date on a trend or a new wave of thinking. It makes me wonder if I should throw in with this project. If you don't know what's happening, odds are your script may be lacking in other areas, too.

Only one cure for that: get up-to-date. Drop in occasionally on the latest goings-on in worlds other than your own. You might even find some thought-starting nuggets that inspire you to other stories.

What sources do you regularly tune in to just to stay up-to-date and well-rounded? What journals, reading lists, websites, or newsletters keep you being the Renaissance Man or Woman you need to be?

Hey, for me, this justifies buying the occasional issue of *Dwell* Magazine, or browsing through the Science section of Amazon, or checking out that Netflix documentary on a topic outside my ken.

This job lets us keep learning — and that's a perk all by itself.

10,000 HOURS
August 3, 2009

I love writers. And I especially enjoy helping young writers who email with the big question: When? *When* will I sell my first script? *When* will I "get on the boards"? My patient reply is always the same: Don't worry about that right now. Have fun! The most important thing to do is to love what you're doing. That way, getting better at it isn't a struggle, it's a pleasure.

One of the surest measures of "when?" has come to us in Malcolm Gladwell's latest book, *Outliers*, a fascinating study of success and what it takes to be successful. As we might suspect, many factors for success include "luck," and Gladwell has given us surprising anecdotes to support his theories.

Did you know, for instance, that the month you were born may be the key to your being a success in Canadian Hockey? Statistically, more star hockey players are born in the early part of the year. It leads to getting up on your skates and playing faster, and dominating others who are born later in the year. And once you dominate Year One of your young career, it pretty much stays that way.

But the one part of Gladwell's book I really appreciated concerned how luck meets opportunity — and the importance of hard work. It's the "10,000 hour rule" Gladwell discovered. That's about how much time anyone must log at a particular skill before he or she starts to get good at it.

Gladwell cites the success of The Beatles as not just being "in the right place at the right time" when they were discovered in

Liverpool, but the many nights they played music, sometimes day and night, while on tour in Germany. What made them great wasn't just their unique musical style, but the mastery of many styles, over many days and months, by the time the call of fame finally came.

Gladwell has the same to say for Bill Gates, Steve Jobs, and other pioneers of the software/Internet/ computer era. It wasn't just that each of these guys was born roughly the same year — or close enough — but that by the time the call came, their "hobby" and fascination with it had absorbed many, many hours of their young lives. How many hours?

About 10,000.

The good news for us is this kind of mileage can be logged not just in writing, but in helping others with their scripts, too — which is why I so heartily recommend the "small group" model of writers getting together and critiquing each others' scripts. Fixing not just your script, but hearing the problems of others, counts too. As does time spent studying movies — and discovering what makes them tick.

It is also the one thing we can control at any age — the time spent to get good at it. Concentrated, focused effort to understand story, character, and execution of ideas — in all forms of communication — makes us the steely pros we need to be when we're called upon to take the place of the star of the show and are told "You're on!"

That, and 10,000 hours, really helps!

HOW DO I KNOW MY SCRIPT IS DONE?
May 26, 2009

Another fantastic workshop this past weekend. And another great question from a writer in class:

How do we know when our scripts are "done"?

Is it the number of drafts?

Is it adoring comments from readers?

Is it how it "feels"?

The answer is: All of the above. And more.

Readers of *Save the Cat!* know I am big into feedback. From the moment we have an idea and wonder if it's any good, to when we write Fade Out, I believe in "call and response" — namely the importance of testing and getting impressions from strangers and friends who hear it all cold.

I also think of *Save the Cat!* as "permission screenwriting." The ability to be clear isn't a slam dunk. And while we writers know what we mean, do others? There's only one way to find out: get permission to continue based on passing each test. The idea of these gated steps is vital to success:

Step One: Is it a good idea? Step Two: Can I say it easily? Step Three: Can we "beat out" this idea to deliver a basic story? Step Four: Do these 15 beats expand to 40 Key Scenes? At any stage of the game we can "drop the ball" too, and discover something in our story needs retooling, so it's also a process with checks and balances — if we're open to them.

I'm your Green Screenwriting Helper: I believe in saving trees as well as cats.

I vote we take into account further steps that help bring an idea to life that makes a script stronger:

— Write a first draft then set it aside. Coming back "fresh" a week later is often a shock, but vital!

— Have not only a coterie of readers who understand, but ones that don't. Like a pitch, it's the strangers who know nothing of us, or the arc of our struggle to succeed, that often have much to tell us.

— And even when you have a draft that "feels" right, I suggest you take it one step further: Have a reading. Gather the thespians in your life and make a pot o' spaghetti for an after-read treat. Bring a tape recorder, too, to catch the nuance of lines that work, and don't work. And poll the actors afterward to get feedback on how they approached the character and either understood — or didn't.

Little Miss Sunshine was 100 drafts to get to final shooting script, and even then, further changes were made on set; yet it was the first draft of *The Verdict* that was the basis of its greenlight, so the number of drafts isn't always a guide. It's good to know that you're ready for whatever it takes.

IT'S WHAT THE PROS USE
July 13, 2009

Recently, I've had the honor of helping out on a couple of studio projects.

For you and I writing on spec, there is a palpable need for success, but get inside the walls of the studio, with millions of dollars and the jobs of your fellows on the line, and the pressure is intense.

So why was I surprised to see the very same tools and techniques we use in play?

When we start getting into it, those same visuals found in our *Save the Cat!* software, and the same phrases and approaches we use in class, lift the development process, too.

"Come over here and look at what we've got so far," I hear before being shown... The Board! And there it is on the studio wall, just like the one I use at home.

To illustrate the direction where we stand with the film in progress, The Board is the *tool* that is whipped out, and it illustrates the story perfectly. "Here we are in the Set-Up of our film, here's our Midpoint, here's our Fun and Games section," and to tell what happens in each scene... a simple declarative sentence.

See! Simple is good. The pros don't have time for less.

And that's not all.

Just like in our Beats and Board classes, the ideas that pop, the understanding of story, and the way we make our point is the same, too.

"Okay, this isn't it, here's the bad way to do this but..." is the way the pros begin their pitch.

That simple preamble to an idea says: "No this may not be it yet, but maybe this direction will jar loose the real way to find the answer."

Because when you are deep in it, looking at the picture in a new way is a must — and really, there is no such thing as a "bad idea." The pros insist on the freedom to be wrong

And I must say that what really makes my heart sing is also the attitude with which the pros take on the task, for it too is just like in our classroom.

It's ever positive. And always moving toward the light.

Yes, we had to give up this whole way of looking at the story that we spent months on... but look how far we came because of it! Look what going down the wrong road helped us find!

We're excited! We are on it! There is an answer here.

And it's fun! Despite all the pressure, man this is the greatest thing I'll ever be involved in... ever!

For writers yet to get their first sale, who think the process is somehow more magical inside the walls than out, no, it's the same. And I am reminded again of some other very important qualities: how ego must be checked at the door, how positivity must be embraced, and how "never give up" must be our motto and the life blood coursing through our veins.

But we knew all this already. Didn't we?

OTHER BOOKS ON STORY AND SCREENWRITING
August 11, 2008

I am often asked if, other than my own books, I recommend any others for readers interested in writing.

Yes! is my happy answer.

I love books on writing, and I'm always inspired by them. And I've used many in my own career to get a better grasp on my work.

Of course, there is the master, Syd Field, and his classic, *Screen-play*. Where would any of us be without this brilliant insight into structure and story? Syd Field is the godfather of screenwriting methodology. And a close second is John Truby whose long awaited book, *The Anatomy of Story*, encapsulates his theories.

I also love Viki King's book *How To Write a Movie in 21 Days* — and used it to write and sell a script in the titular time frame. My other favorites include David Trottier's *Screenwriter's Bible* and any book by Karl Iglesias (either *101 Habits of Successful Screenwriter* or *Writing for Emotional Impact* — both big favs!).

For theory, there is nothing better than a couple you may have heard of, and ones that are on my shelf at the ready: *The Uses of Enchantment* by Bruno Breitleheim and *The Art of Dramatic Writing* by Lajos Egri are ones I often read just for fun — and to get inspired about how fairy tales and folk tales still inform us.

And as far as books about the business are concerned, I still reference both *Hello, He Lied* by Lynda Obst, *Breakfast with Sharks* by Michael Lent, and the classic *Memo* by David O. Selznick (which shows how the more things change, the more they stay the same). These are insider looks at Hollywood, all fun reads.

Recently there is a whole new batch of future classics. Tops on my list is my buddy Will Akers' book, called bluntly, *Your Screenplay Sucks!* Will's wonderful treatise is chock full of things I've always wanted to point out to writers about their scripts, and covers everything from unclear thinking to bonehead mistakes we screenwriters make that scream out: Don't buy my script! Yes, I'm prejudiced, but Will's book is great.

I also really like *Cinematic Storytelling* by Jennifer Van Sijll. Both her book and Will Akers' are found in my current publisher's stable. Michael Wiese Publishing has really cornered the market on the best books out there for entertainment, on every subject from script to directing and producing to post-production.

This goes for my other Michael Wiese favorite author, Michael Hauge, whose most recent MWP book, *Selling Your Story in Sixty Seconds* is absolutely fantastic, and a great companion to Michael's classic *Writing Screenplays That Sell*. Also in the MWP family now is Linda Seger, whose new book is *And The Best Screenplay Goes To...* which covers five award-winning screenplays, and how they got that way.

And of course for pure inspiration, I always pick up *On Writing* by Stephen King, *Bird by Bird* by Anne Lamott, and, believe it or not, the poetry of T.S. Elliot, William Butler Yeats, The Bible (King James edition), and any novel by Vladimir Nabokov, F. Scott Fitzgerald, or Charles Bukowski. For some reason, the joyful use of language — juicy, lip-smacking words on a page — make me want to run to the word processor.

I hope this list is inspiring. What inspires you? That is the question! Inspire me and I will write great, lovely stories and screenplays, and build them into an empire of word pictures that stand...

... forever!

CHAPTER 10

February 8, 2007
"And when you wake up, start singing, damn it.
It's the joy that lets us know we're on the right track."

Inspiration came so naturally to Blake.

THE MAGIC OF DOING THE RIGHT THING
February 8, 2007

Writing *STC!* and teaching my method to others has been the best experience of my life.

Those words flow so easily — and with joy.

I wake up singing most days. I zip over to my computer to answer email from writers I've met (or haven't yet) — and now get to assist. I write my 1000 words a day. I meet with other writers who are working on projects. I get out there and seek opportunities. But in fact the opportunities seek me.

Why?

Because I am doing the thing I was meant to do.

I look back on my whole career and realize that my greatest joy was always helping other writers and being, for lack of a better term, an enthusiast. And the sweet spot of that sweet spot was always talking about story. Even more than writing on my own or with a partner, learning about story has always been my passion. This may not be the career I set out to have, but it's me. And with what we are doing with *STC!*, I feel personally like a lifetime of braking devices, governors of what it's "supposed to look like" that have held me back, are gone, and I am finally free.

I bring this up not to cause you to roll your eyes and say, "How very nice for you Blake... Get the net for Mr. Snyder!" but to take note of the fact that when you are on the right track, things happen.

Are you bucking the system, swimming against the river, or swimming with it? Is this writing thing a joy? Do you get up every day singing, wondering what new tidbit you are going to learn about your story or your career? Are opportunities coming to you?

Take your temperature on this.

Sometimes we stand in our own way and are the ones blocking our best self from coming out due to fear or some pre-conceived notion of how it's supposed to look. If so, let go. Take a break. Take a walk. Take a nap.

And when you wake up, start singing, damn it. It's the joy that lets us know we're on the right track.

LONDON REDUX
October 2, 2006

Finding your bliss is how Joseph Campbell describes it, "realizing your Personal Legend" is what Paulo Coelho says in a wonderful book called *The Alchemist* — and I have found my place talking and thinking about story. And I appreciate those who indulge me on this and allow me to express myself in this way. Please excuse me while my feet leave the ground. I'll be back in a minute!

We tell stories because we must, because we are little tuning forks divining wisdom from beyond. They are the same tales, told again and again over centuries, but we like and need to hear them, and there's a very good reason: because they let us know that when we get up every morning life is worth it. And it is.

Keep at it. Don't stop.

IT STARTS WITH A MAP...
January 1, 2007

Over the holiday I was watching my favorite movie ever: *Lawrence of Arabia*.

I saw something this time (enhanced in later versions of this classic)... it all starts with a map.

After his motorcycle mishap, when we first meet Peter O'Toole as Lawrence in Cairo, he is in the basement of British headquarters, looking at a map of Arabia and its surroundings. Geography plays a big part in this monumental tale, particularly helpful when Lawrence decides to attack Aqaba "... from the land."

This initial scene with Lawrence hovering over a geographic snapshot of what will become the landscape of our story, shows how an overview and knowledge of what we can expect "out there" is vital. In the film, and in history (by coincidence I am re-reading *Seven*

Pillars of Wisdom by T.E. Lawrence), the secret of Lawrence's success was knowledge of the terrain… and having a plan. And we should all follow his example.

What is our plan?

Do we have a set goal of how many scripts we are going to write? A set number of new contacts we are going to make? What can we do with our knowledge of the landscape to change events to our advantage? And what do we hope to accomplish by journey's end? It all starts with a map.

Take a moment to "beat out" the plot points of your year ahead. What do you expect to happen out there, and what can you do to make it happen?

WORKING OUT DA KINKS
March 6, 2007

The Master Class was in session this past weekend.

This is where we take the logline and 15 beats of your movie idea, and we put it up on the dreaded Board — aka The Rack, aka The Wailing Wall — and proceed to beat on it until we get the 40 scenes you need to start writing.

We call it breaking the story, but really it's about finding it. If you want to really do this job, you have to do it. You must work it the same way it's always been worked. In a room. Staring at the board. Drinking coffee. And saying: "I'm not satisfied yet, there's something wonky about the middle; let's see if we can find a better way to raise the stakes."

There's no crying in baseball and no crying in screenwriting either. Give up your darlings! Leave your pre-conceived notions at the door. Be willing to see it a whole new way. And when you do, miracles happen. Bigger, better stories appear. And solutions get found.

Often it's an 11th Hour fix. I think I am most proud of those. For instance, this Sunday at our beat sheet workshop, our little minds turned to jello, looking at the board of a movie we had seen three times or more during the weekend... when suddenly we felt a nagging urge to do even better. In this case, we came up with a fix for the writer's third act that aligned the whole story and made it make even more sense — and I can't stop thinking about how magical that is!

On the good days, when we have these breakthroughs, I feel like Billy Wilder and Izzy Diamond writing *Some Like It Hot*. They did it, like we do it, like it's always been done: in a little office, staring at each other, and doing the hard work. But if you ask the tough questions, you iron out the trouble spots, and better things come from it. And sometimes at the end of the day you realize you had it all along.

Famously, that's how Wilder and Diamond came up with the final line for their sex-switch comedy. When told that the woman he is going to marry is actually a man, when Jack Lemmon takes off his wig and confesses, Joe E. Brown says, "Well, nobody's perfect." Wilder and Diamond couldn't think of anything better. But we know they tried. Up until they shot the scene, they were still ready to find something even more satisfying.

That's what it's all about.

LOVE EACH OTHER
July 11, 2007

You know I am constantly amazed at the hate I read on the Internet.

Is it me, or has our society become meaner?

I personally abhor the rude, the angry, and those that belittle and tear down.

And yet these seem to be the people most likely to be rewarded in our world.

Are TV shows where hopeful but untalented singers who get "ambushed" by producers funny? Are acerbic bloggers in the guise of being "edgy" or "honest" really the best we can hope for in a discussion? Does anger really aid communication?

I am guilty of not always being polite. I have been acerbic myself in the quest to be entertaining or to simply get attention. And I always regret it. The volume level on hate seems to be turned so high on any given day that sometimes we feel like it's the only way to be heard.

I am suggesting that we turn it down.

Anger is for people who fear. And we have nothing to fear.

A little more love please, a little less attention paid to the mean and the angry — no matter how entertaining.

If it takes being mean to be heard in order to sell a script or a TV show, I'd rather not play.

And I certainly would rather not watch.

THANKSGIVING IN LONDON
November 22, 2007

As I travel the world talking about *Save the Cat!*, I must pause here on Thanksgiving to think about how grateful I am for what has happened this year. I am grateful for all the new friends I've made, and the old friends whom I am closer to than ever. But the thing that I am most grateful for is the bigness of the possibilities available to us.

It literally takes my breath away.

In the first *Save the Cat!* book I talk about how it is written for those who want to "swing for the fences," and that still holds true. The many ways we can be fulfilled as writers and creative individuals are truly amazing. Traveling around the world reminds me of the global market that is available to us, and the many means by which we can communicate and have our vision turned into reality. I grew up with a Dad in the business, who, as an Emmy-winning TV producer still had to deal every day with a marketplace that was quite limited. He had three places to sell to: CBS, NBC, and ABC. If he had a bad meeting with Fred Silverman at CBS, Dad was down to two networks. And that was it.

Compare and contrast to now and we truly can be thankful that there are literally thousands of ways to tell our tales, and more being realized every day.

But as we take a time out, it's a good moment to reflect on where we are in the bigness of our own dreams. Let's take a moment to assess where we are, and what we need to do to get where we're going. I remind myself, too, of the importance of dreaming big. Big old world out here, lots and lots of opportunities, nothing but possibilities.

So have some turkey for me back in the states, dream big, and imagine the home run you are going to hit in 2008.

Can't wait to cheer you on!

HAPPY NEW YEAR!
January 3, 2008

I am so excited 2008 is here. It's going to be your best year ever! And we intend to be there with you, cheering you on to success every step of the way. And when I look at all the opportunities available to us — the only option *is* success!

If you are looking at your career with a "woe is me" attitude, get over it! If you feel that "timing" or "corporations" or "lack of money" or "it's all about who you know" is stopping you from winning, you are just plain wrong. The "system" is not in conspiracy to stop you from creating or seeing any movie you want to make or see. The world of the Indie is alive and well! And so is the big-budget studio flick.

There is room for us all.

There is opportunity EVERYWHERE!

There are diamonds lying at our feet — we just have to pick them up.

Any vision you have, any idea you want to express, any character you want to bring to life, you can.

And this is the year you do it.

So what are you doing sitting there eating corn flakes and reading this blog? Get to work! Write up some ideas and go out and pitch them to startled strangers at Starbucks. Start reading scripts or writing one.

Go to the theaters or go to Netflix (my next movie jag is an Otto Preminger weekend featuring *Laura*, *The Man with the Golden Arm*, and *Bunny Lake Is Missing*), and screen some movies that will help inspire the movie you want to write.

Let's go! Let's make this your best year ever.

It starts with saying: Yes!

Happy New Year!

"YAY! THE STRIKE IS OVER!"

February 14, 2008

The 2007-2008 WGA strike *is* over. Instead of dwelling on the pros and cons of the outcome, I choose to simply be relieved that we are in business again. As you know, I am a "Thank God It's Monday" kinda guy. So this week's news means one thing for sure: We can get on with writing and selling our scripts!

"Yay!" indeed.

What the strike proved to me, and what this last 100 days has really been about, is revealing something we already kind of knew: It is the entrepreneurs who will succeed.

The current networks and studios are still our prime target, but we must be on our toes and always seek new ways to get our stuff sold and made. The world is changing rapidly and we must change with it.

And be delighted! And inspired! And excited by all that that entails!

I say it all the time, I'll say it again: There are more opportunities for writers than there have ever been in history!

This now also includes more business opportunities for smart writers who have enough confidence in their material to know the value of what they have.

You, the writer reading this blog, are the one who must control your own destiny. You cannot rely on anyone else to do it for you. The trick is to know the value of what you offer and to be supported by others who know the same. And how do we do that? By being confident in the basics!

Extraordinary idea. Extraordinary story. Extraordinary execution.

To say "It starts on the page" is not enough. We must know in our hearts the amazing value of what we do and cling to it despite every naysayer and obstacle-thrower who stands between us and the recognition we deserve.

And we must seek out others like ourselves — positive, talented, eager to learn, and eager to succeed — to support us.

It starts with you. The heroes, as I say in class, are those who "dig deep" and have faith. And faith is nothing but belief in outcomes we have seen proven time and again.

I believe in you, your talent, your desire to improve, to seek solutions, and to win! And I believe in the amazing possibilities of our world where thoughts truly become things.

Given all that we have before us, all the chances for success and opportunities for growth, is there any other reaction for us to have but to smile?

So let's get back to our business, the business of creativity. And let's never forget the power of our special gift.

WHAT'S YOUR VECTOR?

February 25, 2008

Here is the definition for my favorite new word:

Vector 1) a quantity that has magnitude and direction and is commonly represented by a directed line segment whose length represents the magnitude and whose orientation in space represents the direction; 2) a course or compass heading especially of an airplane.

I love this term! And not surprisingly, it's one that, for me, relates to storytelling — and to life!

In storytelling, whenever I hear the pitch of the movie you're working on, the first thing I ask about it is: "What does the hero want?"

The hero must be proactive throughout. He must want something — and want it badly! The more someone wants to do something, the more we root for them — as long as we sympathize with them, that is! But it always helps if the hero's want is clear and strongly held. In short, he must have a mission that, to quote our dictionary definition, has "magnitude and direction."

This is all well and good for heroes of our stories. We can manipulate a hero's "wants and needs" and should, because when we do it always makes for a better story.

But then comes the uncomfortable question: If we were the hero of our own story (and we most certainly are), what would we characterize as our own want in life?

What's *our* vector?

What is driving us with "magnitude and direction" to get up each day, open our eyes to the new opportunities offered us, and give our best to fulfill our mission?

Watching the Academy Awards® last night, I was taken by how many people spoke of having imagined themselves standing in front of the world to receive that famous gold statue. The annual Oscar® telecast is always a good time to "account for yourself" for participants in the film business, like going home for Thanksgiving and reporting in to your family on how you're doing, and what goals for the new year you hope to achieve.

And it is clear from last night's show that all of us have a shot at that moment in front of the microphone if we want it.

Diablo Cody, winner of Best Original Screenplay for her script *Juno*, was a first-time screenwriter. Her screenplay represents everything we have discussed when it comes to writing a successful story. It's primal. It gives us "the same thing... only different." It has unique and compelling characters. And it is structured beautifully. In interviews, Cody herself has talked about being self-taught in her screenplay skills. Her ability to write a great story came from what we also recommend — watching a lot of movies! For whether picked up by osmosis or learned in school, the skills we need to win are the same. And Cody had the key ingredient we all need to succeed; she had passion.

She had vector!

It's a good time to assess how we intend to arrive at our ultimate destination like the heroes that we are! In the same way the first day of the New Year gives us a chance to make our resolutions, the day after the Oscars® offers film people a similar moment. Whether your mission is get a sale or get an Oscar®, your passion must be in full stride to succeed. My mission is to bring the concepts of storytelling to anyone who wants them and to assist you in reaching your goal any way I can. That is my vector! And I've never felt better in my whole life about what I'm doing. It gets me bouncing out of bed every day, eager to write you back if you email me, read the script you send me, or prepare for the next talk I'm giving that hopefully will give you even one nugget of information that might make a difference to you.

I have my vector.

What's yours?

I hope that whether your vision is standing up in front of the world to receive a gold statue or just getting a movie made that tickles your fancy... and hopefully tickles others too... that you jump in today with passion, excitement, and the desire to do your very best! If you can, you'll go a long way in making your dream come true — and mine too!

OPPORTUNITY

April 24, 2008

I'm a big believer in positivity.

(I know this surprises you!)

But I think that without some clear cut basics, we cannot attain our goals no matter what our goals may be.

My turn in screenwriting came during the 1988 Writer's Strike. After struggling to get into the WGA, the strike, and lack of non-scab work, sent me back to my hometown. It was just 90 miles away from L.A. but far enough to feel like I'd been exiled to another world. I'd had mixed success in writing. My scripts were all over the place. I had "experimented" with what might now be called the YouTube route by making my own video with friends called *The Blank Show*.

Otherwise I had very little to show for all my hard work.

When my father passed away that year, and the strike ended, I decided this was it. Do or die. I was very broke. But with help from another good pal, producer Tommy Lynch, who hired me to write a number of *Kids Incorporated* episodes, I kept body and soul together. And I had a vision!

I got a desk and an office for cheap in downtown Santa Barbara; I lived on $900 per month; and for some reason I got index cards upon one of which I wrote my goals:

"I have sold a million dollar screenplay. I have a three picture deal. I have an office on the lot."

At the time, this was insane. I had no idea how to do these things. I think at that point, I had an agent, but because of my lack of sale-ability, she was just someone to touch base with occasionally.

I had another index card. Upon this I wrote: "DISCIPLINE — FOCUS — POSITIVE ENERGY"

This, it seemed to me, was a winning triumvirate. But I was making this up as I went, so what did I know?

Discipline meant that I would rigorously work hard every day and meet daily goals. Focus meant I would direct my efforts toward one goal: selling a script. And Positive Energy meant to me, that no matter what the results of my efforts or the day, what the news was, or how the pitch went, I would see only the good.

I become Mr. Glass Half Full.

Within four years I had attained all those goals. It was one day while unpacking my stuff, after moving back to L.A. and into an office on the Disney lot, that I found those cards. *Amazing!* I thought. How clear I had been and how clearly I had achieved each one.

This from a guy who at the time I wrote those out, had to scramble to find change in the cushions of the couch to buy a cup of gourmet coffee once a week — my big treat!

What audacity!

I think those opportunities are there for all of us. And as we look out on the landscape, the more specific we can be, the better. When we target our careers and our scripts, we see a vision that becomes the truth, so it's important to pick well.

And dream big.

What is your discipline? What is your focus? What is your mental outlook?

Mine is posted up on my computer this morning. Brand new. Let's see if vision will meet opportunity... again!

CLOSER

June 19, 2008

Every "no" is one step closer to a "yes."

That's a little motto my producer father taught me. And he knew. He proved that "get up off the mat and hit 'em again" works.

My dad's motto is more than a lesson in persistence; it is a mathematical certainty, and a spiritual one. It means there are x number of "no's" between you and victory, so why not get through them?

And do so with a smile?

Why not look at that "pass," that "no thanks," that "sorry, we already have something like it" as getting closer not farther away from your goal. We are closer every time we even assay the field.

I love this philosophy. It helps me stay in the game when a string of "no's" urges me to quit. We are indeed getting closer each time out.

But we must also ask an important question: closer to what?

You say you are closer, but what does that mean?

What is your goal for today? What is your goal for this month? What is your goal for this year?

Are you getting closer to these goals, or do you have to re-tool, change goals, and figure out a new way?

We are halfway through your best year ever! This is the year you succeed wildly. This is the year you become what you always wanted to be. This is the year, 2008, when all your dreams come true.

What does that look like?

Do you have a clear picture of what you're wearing when the phone call comes? Have you picked out the pool that will be in the backyard of the house you buy with the proceeds from your amazing spec screenplay sale that everyone in town is talking about? Do you know what charity you're going to give to with the money that comes flooding in your door?

The routine of pursuing our goals sometimes becomes exactly that — routine. We write x number of pages per day, send out x number of email queries per month, attend x number of meetings with our writers groups. All good. It's the process.

Yet occasionally we must take a beat and look around. As we push toward our goal, let's pause and assess exactly where we're going.

Failure is not an option for us. We are here to succeed. We are here to get closer to our goals by becoming better in the face of a "no." And that alone is a "yes" I can proudly claim every hour of every day!

How is your year progressing? What is your assessment of how you're doing — and what changes do you have to make either in your goals, or your approach to them, to make this year the best ever?

Mostly, what can we do to help? That's also why we're here. If you need help, ask for it. If you want feedback, get it. Ask for help. And ask for success. Say it out loud, and every "no" will become a "yes."

CLAIM YOUR VICTORY

July 10, 2008

"I don't know if you realize how far you've come in a year."

I said these words to a writer the other day, and when I did I thought "What an understatement!" Flashing back to those initial interactions with her, her progress is obvious — and a bit breathtaking.

When we first met, there was very little to recommend in her ideas or the execution of them.

She wasn't quite getting it. I wondered, frankly, if she ever would. And as a result, no one else was getting it either. No wonder she heard crickets from those agents and producers she sent her scripts and pitches to.

And look now: She has a script being read by a major studio, interest from an agent, and fresh new ideas that have merit — and commercial promise.

All in a year.

This is one of the joys of having my job. I can see your improvement. I can tell you exactly how much better you are at this than when we met.

It's important for us to claim these victories, to occasionally stop and admit that our lives have gotten quantifiably better.

And if you don't believe me, I suggest you create a "Writer's Resume."

What's that?

Occasionally even writers are called upon to account for themselves and the full arc of their careers. I had to do this recently and was astounded at all the stuff I had to cut out to make room for new successes.

The achievement that seemed so big on the last resume seems small by comparison; look how far I've come!

And by the time I finished, I also had the ah-ha! of seeing how the seemingly random flailings I thought were leading nowhere at the time, actually looked planned when seen from a higher perspective. What else could explain how one relationship, job, script, or interaction led me so seamlessly to the next level?

A Writer's Resume also makes us realize our job is unique. We're creatives. Not everything we do can be measured in dollars and cents. I love my sales, and love the achievement of them, but I'm

178 BLAKE'S BLOGS ~ Blake Snyder

proud of every script I've written and looking back can see why I had to write each one — even those that didn't sell.

There are partnerships, ongoing class work, skill sets gained that we can tack on to our Writer's Resume, including the simple realization of how some aspect of writing and storytelling works.

The arc of our development as writers is not just the puffery of a CV that shows the latest thing we can write home about, but the education and experience of a steely pro who, when called on, can deliver.

Would you hire you? What service do you offer that no one else can? What is the poster of you?

These are all questions that creating a Writer's Resume can help you answer, and help you plan for your next level.

I hope mostly that it tickles you to see what a fun ride this is! My Gosh! The odd jobs I had to suffer through early on, writing on the side, at night in 24-hour restaurants, the Moments of Clarity when a sudden breakthrough let me know I was onto something! These victories cannot be measured or fully claimed until we see that there really is a plan, and we are fulfilling it every day! Whether we recognize it or not!

RESISTANCE IS FERTILE!
August 26, 2008

I have been working on a dizzying number of projects of late.

In addition to my own writing, I hear or read dozens of movie ideas, treatments, and scripts every day. And my mental muscle in dealing with them gets a regular workout. Physically, I may need more days at the gym, but mentally I am buff! I am chiseled! I am the Mr. Universe of story solving.

What all this brain exercise is good for is quickness to hear and see problems. This method, the *Save the Cat!* method of telling stories, really works. And it's why the 50-point checklist we've developed in-house to expose any story's weakness is so valuable. If I were a financier with a movie about to go into production, I would make sure I went down that list before any script was given the green light. No matter where your story is, or where you are — from the studio level, to the individual writer — the weak points of a script are the same. And if you are not looking for ways to fix them, the results can only be less than they could be.

If you are not sending your hero all the way back to show all the problems of his world at the beginning, I will send you there to explore them. If you have all action and no meaning, I will make you look at your Theme, and figure out what B Story it ties into, and why it is not connecting to the overall plot.

If you are not delivering on the premise you pitched me, I will ask you to camp out in your Fun and Games section for a while and figure out why you are not giving me the "poster" — and force you to examine the real question: Is your premise not there to begin with?

And of course when I tell you this, very often your reaction is not a happy one.

You had it all worked out! It was perfect! Everyone else liked it! Why, Blake, don't you?

And I can only say one thing in reply, at least in my head: Resistance is futile!

But resistance also builds 12 story muscles 12 ways.

The pushback between you and me is positively gorgeous! We argue and your story begins to build muscles too. It starts to get handsomer and more quick on its feet, and the awkward pause you had while explaining it suddenly goes away because I've forced you to vet yourself, and given you the means to do so, and expose your blind spots, and see the story for what it really is — or isn't.

And after it's all over, and you say, You were right! I smile. I didn't do anything. You did it. I didn't find your fix. I suggested a few. But you did the work. I just pushed back and made you build your own story muscles. Be proud of yourself.

You had the guts to try something new. You dared to give up your "contempt prior to investigation" that so many lesser writers never got over. And now you can stand up taller than before all by yourself.

Resistance, turns out, may be futile, but it's also fertile and gives birth to an amazing array of better stories, better told, and with a better chance not only of selling but succeeding!

AN OPTIMISTIC FORECAST!
October 6, 2008

I'm not a contrarian, but here's my optimistic forecast: keep writing and you will win!

I've received a lot of emails lately from writers asking if they should continue. These are smart writers, who are approaching this very difficult business with a good work ethic, focus, and cool aplomb. But the grind is getting to them. The sound of "one hand clapping" is starting to get unnerving, and Aunt Fern (my mythic relative who always corners me at Thanksgiving to ask "How's the writing going?" — when in fact that's really not what she's asking!) is ever on the periphery, waiting to level her loaded question. We are hardy and resilient folk, but seriously, tick-tock, man, bills to pay, responsibilities to meet, I'm still on it...

But is it worth continuing?

The odds of selling a spec script are long enough to make any reasonable person go pale. How can we continue to compete when the recent headlines from *Variety* show not only a slowdown in the entertainment sector, but also a tendency to go with projects with brand names. They are putting into production a lot more *Tarzans* and sequels, and hiring more veteran creatives with track records. If we neither have a brand, nor a track record worthy of veteran status, maybe giving up is the logical choice?

Yet I remain bullish.

Look for instance at this weekend's #1 at the box office: a fun, friendly, family comedy with a great poster and title, *Beverly Hills Chihuahua*. Family movies almost always do well and there aren't enough of them — and I happen to love them. But the same can be said for horror films, a genre I don't like as a rule. Still, *The Strangers* was such a hit, they're making a sequel, and *Saw* is into its fifth incarnation. Got a snappy comedy? We saw several grabbed up in the past few weeks, a few by first-time writers. And the action movie business is thrilling — is there more of a Dude With A Problem than *Eagle Eye*, last week's #1?

Each of these movies started with something any of us is capable of coming up with: an idea they can't say "no" to. And that is where it all begins — as tried and true a tradition as any entrepreneur must aspire to.

The well-executed, high-concept, smartly-targeted screenplay is gold. Do we have to be more clever at finding partners, attaching talent, and building buzz around our project — yes, absolutely! Do we have to work hard at both our writing skills and our political ones to keep making those valuable contacts? Yes 2.

But in troubled times, the need to be taken away from the day to day grind is our job!

People besides Aunt Fern are counting on us: don't let them down!

WHAT'S YOUR FOCUS?

January 29, 2009

The new year is just getting underway — 2009 is the best ever for our writing careers.

And for many, that means thinking about your writing in a brand new way.

In my forthcoming book, *Save the Cat!® Strikes Back*, my favorite chapter is the last one. It describes the summer I became a "professional writer." The idea that it is a profession seems to offend some people. These are the folks who believe that creativity should not be subject to the same rules as every other venture in life. And I admit, I was like that too, until the summer I gave up being a "bullhead" and began figuring out how to channel my creativity in a way that might be pleasing — and useful — to someone other than just me.

As part of that transformation, I discovered how "keeping business hours" — a set time and place and goal for my work — instead of being restricting, is actually freeing, and far more productive than I ever imagined. I also learned how maintaining a positive attitude, and finding a silver lining in every pitch meeting, phone call, contact, and hiccup in my progress, kept me on track to the ultimate positive outcome.

But my most important discovery was "Focus." This is the idea that I have a specific goal — and even pick a specialty that I make it my business to master.

By choosing a specialty — e.g., I write rom-coms, or horror, or action — it becomes easier to find you, and see you as someone offering a service. Of all the important tools in achieving any goal, this is the key to finding your focus: knowing how others "see" you and trying your best to deliver better every time out.

What's your service? And how is your focus on getting better at it getting you results?

By focusing on what you want to achieve this year, you raise your odds of doing it.

And I will be there with you, rooting for you every step of the way!

GIVE ME THE SAME THING... ONLY BETTER! PART 1
March 3, 2009

There is a famous blooper that caught 1950s TV star, Bozo the Clown, on tape for the ages.

In an unguarded moment at the end of the show, when the famous kiddie host thought the microphones were off, he expressed frustration with his audience, exclaiming: "That oughta hold the little bastards!"

I think of this line occasionally when I consider the perception of Hollywood... and it gives me the willies.

It speaks to an "us" the creators vs. "them" the audience mentality, and an attitude that says: We've met the basic standard for today's entertainment and that should be enough. We've done the job. Let's call it a day.

And I want to go on record right now: This is not the mindset of the most successful in our business, and it should not be ours. But I believe there is a sneaky suspicion by some in our audience that it might be.

If I had one thing to do over again in the writing of *Save the Cat!*® it would be to enhance the helpful advice a studio executive told me during a meeting. "Give me the same thing... only different" was his mantra. It meant the best pitch was something familiar enough to understand but with a new, fresh, and ironic twist.

And that's still good insight into the business.

Storytelling through the ages has forever sought variations on an art which must deal with the well-known fact that there truly is "no new story under the sun." But I prefer: Give me the same thing... only *better!*

Save the Cat!® is a language of storytelling terms and tools — easy and instantly applicable — that "sets the table" for further discussion. That's why I wrote it. Early on, I attended many screenwriting classes (a few well-known ones), read many books, and what I always wanted — but rarely got — was something that would actually HELP me in my career... today... right now. I wanted something I could DO immediately that would resonate not only with audiences, but with the gatekeepers who separated me from the audience.

We have succeeded in "setting the table" and establishing a language to better dissect, understand, and deliver on what makes for solid storytelling. But it does not mean we should stand for the status quo.

We stand for improving skill, focused effort, and hard work beyond the five o'clock whistle. We stand for going the extra mile to make our ideas not just different than what came before... but better. And we must.

Within "the rules" of what makes the film business tick — vital for us to understand — this is only a starting point. Knowing what we know about "poster," structure, transformation, and "stories that resonate," we must seek out in our work something we don't always sense onscreen, with the cameras either off or on:

Excellence.

To succeed beyond our wildest dreams we must push ourselves to new levels of achievement — whether we are writing a silly rom-com, frothy musical, thriller, horror flick, Academy-considered Indie or any other of a thousand "same thing... only different" subjects out there. We must always make sure we wring out every last drop of story, and every bit of enlightenment, excitement, freshness, and beauty we can from ourselves.

Let's make it our goal this year and every year to drive beyond what will "hold 'em" — no matter what our genre, goal, or familiarity with commercial success. Let's make being "better" our guiding light every day.

ARE YOU DELIGHTFUL?

April 9, 2009

"That was delightful!" I said to one of the writers at my workshop a few Sundays ago.

Honestly, I don't know where that word came from. It just sort of slipped out.

But "delightful" was exactly the word to describe the final pitch she gave the class Sunday afternoon. She had worked hard on her story beats, and like others in the class, the gears in her mind were visibly stripping as the notion of the story she had collided with the new method she was learning that weekend.

And yet by the time she stood up and pitched out her story, she did so with enthusiasm. Beneath the surface of the plot points was a joy in telling it, and showing how its pieces all fit together. Isn't this cool? I could almost see in her expression. *And aren't I good at doing this? And knowing that, isn't this fun?*

Delightful. That was the only word for it.

Are you delightful? Quite literally, are you filled with delight as you go about working out the beats of your story? You should be. This story you're working on doesn't have to be a comedy. It can be a deep drama, and it can feel like pulling teeth at times as you try hard to figure out what part fits where — and why you are even putting yourself through this!

But there must be a sly wink you give to yourself in the depths of this process that says: *Yeah! I am mastering this! It's slow, it's tough, it's getting better a millimeter a day, but by God, this is fun!*

Conquering any story must be so. And no matter what story you write, I want to see the gleam in your eye when you pitch it, or sense the joy I can read between the lines of your script that says: *That's right! I'm baaaad!* Because the delight you find is in our faces, too, as we listen to your pitch or read your story in awe.

Delight yourself. And you will delight us.

SAVE THE CAT! GOES TO THE UK
April 9, 2009

I feel fortunate to meet so many writers around the world, and be immersed in so many different storytelling traditions. From my experiences with filmmakers in China this past fall, to the amazing insights I've gleaned from the marvelous members of the Romance Writers of America, to writers I will meet this weekend that include representatives from Spain, Poland, Germany, and France, I continue to be amazed at our common cause. It's because at core what we're involved in, and care vitally about, is trying to grab hold of that elusive glimmer in our imaginations — and wrestle it to the ground.

The more I travel, the more I realize the image of "the writer alone in the room, staring at a blank page" is false — or can be. I believe in the small group. I believe in peer-to-peer feedback. I believe in exchange of ideas and new notions about what "story" is, and incorporating it all! Being part of our common cause, sharing experience and insight, is empowering. But the best part is: We're not alone.

I got an email from an insightful young writer here in the UK yesterday asking "Is the Three Act Structure dead?" To be honest, I told him, I don't understand the question. To me, what storytelling is about is "transformation" and "being touched by the divine" — that's all we care about. And however we frame that, be it three acts or four, multiple story lines, or full-on flashbacks doesn't matter — so long as we deliver on those two key — and universal — requirements. The idea that there is a young writer out there both questioning concepts of structure, and theories about how to make storytelling better, is such a exciting prospect. We keep learning, we keep sharing what we find, and we improve.

So when we do finally get back to our computer screens, or writing pads, or get ensconced with our portables in a coffee shop and are... alone at last... all that beautiful information, and feedback, can be part of the story we are telling. I love being away to gather new thoughts, but love being back at the Wurlitzer keyboard too, alone, thinking about all I've learned, and ready for the next Fade In...

It's the only way to travel.

Blake and his students at a London seminar.

CAT! NATION
March 30, 2009

We are a band of writers, creators, innovators, seekers, and gurus.

We span the globe from China, Australia, Canada, Israel, Japan, South Africa, and France to Germany, Poland, Italy, Spain, the US, India, and the UK.

The power of what we offer is awesome. We are storytellers and poets, filmmakers and advertising whiz kids, marketing geniuses, romance writers, horror aficionados, action junkies, hardcore dramatists, and musicians.

You harness this energy and we can save your cineplex, sell your innovative car that is only an idea on a drawing board, write a better resume. We can frame the argument in a way that grabs you, and makes you cry or laugh or think... at will.

We are working in your basement, at the next table in your corner coffee shop, in the bus going down your street, early in the morning, on a break at lunch, and late at night while everyone else is sleeping.

We are armed and ready with the most dangerous weapon on this earth: the truth. And we are forging new ideas right now in the orange-hot furnace of our imaginations, pounding on the iron to sharpen the edges, ignoring the heat in favor of the light, and the sparks, and the danger of creating something a little scary.

It's easy. And it's hard. And it's beautiful. And it's hard. And it's lovely. And it's breathtaking. And it's hard.

And we love it.

We love it because you cannot take it away from us. Because it's ours, our way, at least for now.

And we are learning more every day, and chalking up experience, and insight, and talent, and tips for what works and what doesn't, and even a bad day is a great day, because no matter what happens to what we make, if we just push our knowledge forward one little bit, we retain the wisdom of what we have learned.

And any minute we will walk up to you smiling, and plop down the clipping of our latest triumph, or deliver the pages that are now suddenly bound between two covers, or hand you a ticket for the show we made.

We will show you our cards that we've been holding all along, and let you know why we were smiling.

Because we have been building something all along, a monument that cannot be torn down.

It is as glorious as glorious gets and we're just doing our job… the one we were meant to do.

We are unherd-able and yet we are everywhere!

Me-freekin'-ow!

THANK YOU!
October 3, 2007

I just wanted to send out a special note of gratitude to everyone who's touched my life.

So often we are concerned with "getting ours" that we don't realize how much we already gots.

And the most special gift I have received is the friendship, love, and support of my friends, family, and fellow writers I have met in the past few years, and all the people who've been my friend since we first said "Hi!"

This means you.

We don't often get a chance to thank those who contribute so much to our lives in small and big ways and make our lives what we are.

You have made mine.

Our friendship is what this life is about. We are all of us muddling along, trying our best, moving ahead despite getting distracted by the victories that swell our heads and the defeats that leave us shivering in the dark at 3 a.m. We get so caught up in brushing the burs off our clothes that we don't realize we are standing in the middle of a bright field of flowers.

And we often miss the point.

It's about helping each other, and being there for each other, and lending our experience, our strength, and our hope to each other until we can march on.

And you do that for me.

So THANK YOU! for all you do to make my life a gift.

Thank you for the wit, wisdom, and joy you've lent me when I needed it most.

Thank you for being AMAZINGLY special in the most AMAZINGLY simple ways!!

Today, as Gary Cooper said in *Pride of the Yankees*, I feel like I'm the luckiest man-man-man on the face of the Earth-Earth-Earth...

*"I look back on my whole career and realize that my greatest joy
was always helping other writers."*

February 8, 2007

SAVE THE CAT!®
GOES TO THE
INDIES

The Screenwriters Guide to 50 Films from the Masters

COMING
APRIL 2017

SALVA RUBIO
BASED ON THE BOOKS BY
BLAKE SNYDER

COMING
FALL 2018!

Artwork Not
Final

SAVE THE CAT!®
WRITES
A NOVEL

BY JESSICA BRODY

Based on the bestselling
screenwriting books by
Blake Snyder

TEN SPEED PRESS

WORKSHOPS
BOOKS
SOFTWARE
SAVE THE CAT!®

Printed in Great Britain
by Amazon